The story of Ernest  h
and humour; in h
Jesus and tireless of
salvation to his Je nd
will be to all those who .... eat
read.

Helen Shapiro

Mike Moore rightly records that the number of lives Ernest
Lloyd touched for good...cannot be counted. I am among
them. In my teens I tried never to miss a meeting when Ernest
came to Dublin, and, for two memorable hours, he counselled
me on the future course of my life. I have revelled in this
book – laughing over Ernest's inimitable typing, shedding
quiet a tear over Jessie's death, and always standing in very
loving awe of a giant among the servants of the Lord Jesus.
Let him be your teacher and example as he has been mine!

Alec Motyer

With Ernest Lloyd's vast experience of mission spanning seven
decades, little wonder for many in Scotland and beyond,
Christian Witness to Israel is simply 'Mr Lloyd's mission'.
Like Caleb at 85, five years his junior, Ernest Lloyd's energy
and authority has waned little with the passing of the years.
Mike Moore's sparkling biography brings this remarkable
career to life. The book will enthral and captivate readers
with the amazing story of God's transformation of a Jewish
orphan boy into the undoubted international authority on
Jewish missions that he is today. I unreservedly recommend
this book as a wonderful celebration of a life still lived to the
glory of God.

Rev. John S. Ross
Greyfriars Free Church of Scotland, Inverness

The
Importance
of being
Ernest

A Jewish Life spent in Christian Mission

Mike Moore

Christian Focus/
Christian Witness to Israel

Cover photo of Ernest Lloyd 1937
All photos courtesy of C.W.I.

Copyright © Mike Moore 2003

ISBN I 85792 806 7

Published in 2003 by
Christian Focus Publications, Geanies House,
Fearn, Tain, Ross-shire, IV20 ITW, Scotland

www.christianfocus.com

and

Christian Witness to Israel, I66 Main Road,
Sundridge, Sevenoaks, Kent, TNI4 6EL

Cover design by Alister MacInnes

Printed and bound by
Cox & Wyman, Reading, Berkshire

Contents

This book is dedicated to the memory of
Jessie Lloyd. Without her unwavering
commitment to the Lord Jesus Christ, there
would have been no life of Ernest to write.

Acknowledgements

It has long been an ambition of mine to write a great book; but I'm afraid this is not it. It is, however, a book about a great man that does not even begin to do justice to him.

I have known and respected Ernest Lloyd for almost twenty years and during this project my respect and admiration have deepened. At times the regard I have for him has verged on awe. Ernest is a preacher, teacher, missionary, evangelist, soul winner and a leader of men. He is equally at home speaking to a handful of people in a living room as he is preaching at an international convention. I have tried in this modest offering to pay tribute to a great man, an important man in the realm of Jewish mission and the Hebrew Christian/ Messianic Jewish world. I hope that in some small way I have succeeded.

Throughout his life Ernest has read and preached from the Authorised (King James) Version of the Bible, therefore all Scriptural quotations in the following pages are taken from the AV.

This book would never have seen the light of day without the encouragement and help of a considerable number of people. Several CWI supporters sent anecdotes, reminiscences and tributes. Not all could be included in the book but I am grateful to all who sought to help me with their contributions.

I am, of course, grateful to Ernest, who allowed me to stay at his home for a week and gave unsparingly of his time throughout the project. John Ross, who was CWI's General Secretary at the time of writing, pushed me into the project, stayed on my back and (for reasons known only to himself) had "every confidence" that I could not only write the book but also complete it on time. Davida Woodman transcribed most of the tapes of my interviews with Ernest, and Jonathan Foo scanned many of Ernest's reports from the BJS Missionary Herald. Elmstead Baptist Church kindly allowed me to shut myself away in the church office and use the office computer for weeks on end in the spring of 2002, and Mary Day supplied coffee and Kit Kats whenever she was in the office. Sarah Edmonds allowed me to use her PC in the summers of 2001 and 2002 and some of the final chapters were completed on the computer of my nephew Adam Horscraft.

John Steinbeck once wrote, "No one wants advice – only corroboration". However, I have been grateful for both the advice and criticism of others. Margaret Jones volunteered to read the manuscript and my secretary, Janet Smith, read each draft. Both made valuable observations and many of their suggestions were incorporated into the final text. Any remaining errors – grammatical or factual – are entirely mine. Although he probably doesn't know it, Viv Thomas was a constant encouragement; our occasional lunches at Starbucks were oases of spiritual refreshment at times when I was feeling the strain. William MacKenzie of Christian Focus Publications was very gracious and extended the deadline for the book several times!

Finally, I have to thank Jenny who stayed married to me in spite of the fact that she spent holidays alone and had to

Acknowledgements

paint the dining room and extension of our house on her own while I was locked away with a computer. She also made time to read the first draft of the manuscript and gave advice, criticism and encouragement. She knew I could, even when I thought I couldn't.

Mike Moore
November 2002

I
Bereshith: in the beginning

*And I will bring the blind by a way
that they knew not.* (Isaiah 42:16)

In *Guard the Gospel,* his exposition of 2 Timothy, evangelical leader John Stott writes: "The most formative influence on each of us has been our parentage and our home. Hence good biographies never begin with their subject, but with his parents, and probably his grandparents as well."

While that is generally true, in the case of Ernest Lloyd neither of his parents played a major part in the most formative years of his life. He never knew his father and at the age of five he was placed in the care of the Naomi Home for Women and Children, run by the Barbican Mission to the Jews. Therefore, the formative influences on Ernest were Christian workers.

His father was killed during the First World War and Ernest's only recollection of his mother is that of a tall, dark, Italian Sephardi Jewess, from whom he probably inherited his height, black hair and striking looks. Why she placed her son in the care of Christians remains a mystery, but life was hard in the years of the First World War, particularly for a young Jewish widow and her son. Jews were lumped together with the Germans and treated as though they were enemy agents.

The popular view of the Jews of England was not without its historical antecedents. Edward I expelled the Jews from England in 1290, but in 1656 the Lord Protector, Oliver Cromwell, influenced by Puritan theology, readmitted them. In contrast to the Roman Catholic Church, the Puritans did not view the Jewish people primarily as "Christ-killers". Familiarity with the Scriptures led the majority of Puritan divines to hold the Jewish people in high regard, believing that although they were outcasts from their own land, there would one day be a national restoration to divine favour and the bulk of the nation would be converted to faith in their Messiah. John Owen, who was arguably the greatest of all the Puritan theologians, wrote of the Jewish nation in his magisterial commentary on the Epistle to the Hebrews:

> They shall return to their own land; they shall enjoy it for a quiet and everlasting possession, their adversaries being destroyed; they shall also be filled with the light and knowledge of the will and worship of God, so as to be a guide and blessing to the residue of the Gentiles who seek after the Lord, and perhaps, shall be entrusted with great empire and rule in the world. The most of these are foretold concerning them, not only in their own prophetic writings, but also by the divine writers of sundry books of the New Testament. But all this we say must come to pass, when the veil shall be taken from their eyes, and when they shall look on him whom they have pierced, and when they joyfully receive him whom they have sinfully rejected for so many generations.

In his comments on Romans II, the Puritan Bible commentator Matthew Henry urged his Christian readers to love the Jewish people, and expressed his confidence that the national conversion of the Jewish people would have far reaching consequences for the gentile nations and the church:

> Now two things he exhorts the Gentiles to, with reference to the rejected Jews:- To have a respect for the Jews, notwithstanding, and to desire their conversion. This is intimated in the prospect he gives them of the advantage that would accrue to the church by their conversion, Rom. II:12, 15. It would be as life from the dead; and therefore they must not insult or triumph over those poor Jews, but rather pity them, and desire their welfare, and long for the receiving of them in again.

As England's reputation for prosperity and religious tolerance spread, increasing numbers of Jews began arriving in the country. Among the Jews to be welcomed as a result of the new openness were the Sephardim, Spanish Jews seeking asylum from the persecutions of the Roman Catholic Church.

Though the Jews established themselves once again in English society, throughout the eighteenth century they had no civil rights and were regarded as "aliens". Jews were barred from trading in the City of London, and because the taking of a Christian oath was required in order to enter university or to practise law, Jewish people were thereby excluded from most professions.

In 1858 Jews were finally accorded full civil rights, culminating in the freedom to vote and to stand for election to the House of Commons. When Benjamin Disraeli became the first Jewish prime minister in 1868, he likened his achievement to having climbed to the top of a greased pole. As a result of severe outbreaks of anti-Semitism in Eastern Europe during the nineteenth century, Ashkenazi Jews began to arrive in Britain. Between 1880 and 1914 some 100-150,000 Eastern European Jews settled in Britain, around 100,000 in London alone. Entire communities uprooted and regrouped in Whitechapel and Stepney.

The residents of the East End feared that the newcomers would swamp them and the Jews quickly became convenient scapegoats for whatever ills befell the country. If unemployment rose, it was because the Jews were taking all the jobs; if rents increased, Jewish immigration was to blame. Hatred and suspicion of the outsiders was further fuelled by the theology of the Catholic Church. Not only were these foreigners, with their strange customs and Eastern European accents, taking the jobs of Englishmen, they were also "Christ-killers". As a consequence, Jewish children found themselves embroiled in bitter squabbles and fights in school playgrounds, and certain streets became "no-go" areas that the Jews avoided for fear of violence. Such was the world into which Ernest Lloyd was born on 13th March 1913, in the West London borough of Hammersmith.

The organisation behind the Naomi Home, into whose care Ernest was placed, came into being in 1879 in the Barbican district of London as "an agency for gospel work among the Jews conducted by Hebrew Christians", and in 1891 became the Barbican Mission to the Jews. The work of the society expanded to other cities in the UK, Palestine and Eastern Europe, where, in Poland particularly, many Jews responded in faith to the message of the Jewish Messiah. William Wingate, a missionary to the Jews of Budapest, wrote in the 1920s, "Hebrew Christians are everywhere. Every class of Jewish society contributes these converts—professors in universities, lawyers, medical men, literary men, musicians, artists, merchants, mechanics, poor and rich are quickened by the Spirit of all grace, convinced of their sin and guilt. They are at the feet of Jesus, and enabled to say with every believer, 'We have redemption through the atoning blood of Jesus, even the forgiveness of our sins'."

The director of the Barbican Mission to the Jews at the time Ernest entered Naomi was the Rev. C.T. Lipshytz, a Polish Jew who had been born into a Hasidic family in Warsaw in 1845. Hasidism was an emotional and ecstatic form of Judaism which originated in Eastern Europe in the eighteenth century, centred around charismatic leaders known as *zaddikim*, or righteous ones. The most notable *zaddik* was Israel ben Eleazar, known popularly as the Baal Shem Tov, meaning "Master of the Good Name". Hasidism was initially rejected by mainstream Jews as fanatical and heretical, but with its emphasis on emotion and joy, in the oppressive climate of violent anti-Semitism, the movement spread quickly.

Lipshytz began to study the Christian faith at the age of thirteen, some time after his older sister had become a believer in Jesus. Her consistent and faithful testimony impressed him deeply, and after he was himself convinced that Jesus was the Messiah promised in the Hebrew Scriptures, he was baptised and changed his name from Hayyim (Life) to Christlieb (Love of Christ) Traugott (Trust in God). His father was so crushed by what he considered to be his son's act of treachery, that to the day of his death twenty years later, he refused to forgive him.

Christlieb Traugott Lipshytz arrived in London in 1887, and two years later he was appointed director of the society that was to become the Barbican Mission to the Jews. Under Lipshytz's direction the work grew and expanded. A medical mission was established in the East End of London and on

27th March 1909, Lady Napier opened the Naomi home at 85 Trinity Road, Tooting, which provided accommodation for up to twenty-five children. Anyone who has tried to negotiate Tooting High Road and Trinity Road by car will hardly recognise the description of the area in *Immanuel's Witness*, the "Quarterly Record of the Barbican Mission to the Jews". Lipshytz wrote that the air "is beautifully fresh, and it is impossible to exaggerate the boon it is to us to have such a place to which we can send weak, delicate, and jaded women and children from the crowded streets and courts of London."

Also taking part in the opening ceremony were evangelical dignitaries Sir Robert Anderson and Sir Andrew Wingate. Although Anderson is best known today for his influential book, *The Coming Prince*, for a number of years he held a senior office at Scotland Yard, the headquarters of the Metropolitan Police. In 1888, when the East End of London was in the grip of Jack the Ripper's reign of terror, Anderson was appointed Assistant Commissioner of Metropolitan Police and Chief of the Criminal Investigation Department. He successfully directed this work until his retirement in 1901 and during his term in office crime in London decreased significantly.

Immanuel's Witness recorded that in her prayer Lady Napier pleaded that God "would in every way bless the new Home they were opening that afternoon: bless it to the mothers who would perhaps be there in times of sickness, and bless it to the children who were brought there that they might learn there was One above Who loved and cared for the children, and Who would watch over them and protect them. She hoped the Home would extend the Kingdom of God amongst Jewish women and children."

Her prayer was to be answered abundantly in the coming years and particularly so in the life of a child who was at that time unborn. Ernest Lloyd came into the world almost four years to the day after Lady Napier's prayer, and when at the age of five he came under the care of Naomi, the home was filled to capacity.

The aim of the home was "to instruct the little ones in the Gospel of Christ, and to break down, in the most effectual manner possible, the walls of relentless prejudice which Rabbinism has erected around the lives of Jewish boys and girls." *Immanuel's Witness* of September 1912 explained:

> The children are… placed in circumstances which will make "all the difference" in regard to their after-lives. Some of them are orphans; others have but one parent, who is unable to pay adequate attention to their up-bringing. Where, in the past, there may have been neglect and want, now, along the lines of a simple economy, there is provision for daily need, combined with a homely care in regard to moral and spiritual well being… As to the convalescents, they are little folk who, for the want of a few weeks careful treatment, might become invalids for life. In some cases a small payment is made on behalf of those whom we have in charge; and having no desire to pauperise honest people, we take such payment without hesitation. Needless to say, on admission, we find it necessary, generally speaking, to apply soap and water in a measure that had not hitherto been customary, also to supply suitable clothing. Then, in a few days, we see results: the little wan faces show a vigorous complexion, and one and another of the company "becomes a picture of health".

In spite of the obvious wellbeing of the Naomi children, the Jewish Press did not take kindly to the avowed aims of the home's founders. *The Jewish World* of 10th May 1914 raged: "Is it true that Jewish children are being committed to the care of the Mission to be brought up as Christians? Is it true that several young people have been received into the Church of Christ by holy baptism? If it is true, then it is a burning shame upon our community, which does not prevent it".

Ernest's mother probably became aware of the existence of Naomi through the Barbican's clinic and dispensary on the Whitechapel Road. In pre-National Health Service Britain, free health care was available for the needy through a number of Christian medical missions, including the Barbican. The Barbican Medical Mission was established some forty years before the NHS, and during 1914 treated 8,707 patients, 2,086 of whom were new cases. In the preceding year the total number of cases was 7,297. There were other free dispensaries in the East End, but according to the Barbican's Medical Officer Dr J. MacNaught Scott, "Our patients are not merely so many cases to be treated, but souls to be saved".

Two letters, both from the same father and written to the Barbican Director a year apart, illustrate that some children found their way into Naomi by way of the Medical Mission. They also reveal the desperation that forced some Jewish parents to place their children in the care of a Christian mission. No doubt Ernest's mother was driven by equally dire straits to place her beloved child in the Naomi Home.

March 2nd, 1914.

DEAR SIR, – I hope you will pardon me for the liberty I take in addressing you, but I have a case to lay before you that I will endeavour to explain. The facts are these:– just over fourteen years ago I was married to a non-Jewess, and we have had a family of five children. Unfortunately my wife and her last child died seven weeks ago. I am now left with four children – the eldest a boy of twelve and the youngest a girl of four. I haven't a relative of mine or my wife's to see to the children, and they are practically in a deplorable condition.

I have been thinking of applying to the Jewish authorities for help, but I am reluctant to do so. I would sooner they be brought up in the Christian faith, if possible, because they are neither one or the other. I happened to pass your [Medical Mission] in Whitechapel on Saturday, and being placed as I am, I thought of appealing to you first. As for myself, I could tell you more personally, only I should like to know whether my case is eligible for relief.

I earnestly trust that you can find it convenient to let me know, as I am in a terrible plight with the children, having nobody to look after them. I must draw to a close. Trusting to hear from you, I remain,

Yours respectfully,

March 16, 1915.

DEAR MR. LIPSHYTZ, – It is just over a year since I first applied to the Barbican Mission in reference to my motherless children; and after surveying the past twelve months, I feel that I should be lacking in my duty as their father if I did not express my gratitude for your goodness towards me and my children. Therefore, Mr. Lipshytz, will you kindly convey to the Committee of the Barbican Mission my heartfelt and sincere gratitude for the manner in which (through you) they came to my aid.

As I look back and think of what might have befallen my children and what they are now, thanks to the Barbican Mission, I am drawn to the conclusion that it is the work of Divine Providence placed you in my path.

I trust that the Barbican Mission will continue the work, and there is no doubt of it whilst they have your able and wise counsel.

I remain, Yours with best wishes,

*****

By today's standards, life at Naomi was hard. Each child slept in a dormitory with three or four others. Children as young as six and seven had to rise early, make their beds and do their appointed chores, which included tasks such as cleaning shoes and polishing the stove. The closest thing to a summer holiday was a walk to Wandsworth Common.

Ernest's recollection of the "wholesome diet" referred to in *Emmanuel's Witness* is of a breakfast of watery, lumpy porridge and a slice of bread and margarine. If anything was left, it reappeared at lunch and tea time until every scrap was consumed. Lunch was an equally Spartan repast of nondescript meat accompanied by over-boiled potatoes and whatever vegetables were available. As a special treat, the children enjoyed the luxuries of cake and jam once a fortnight.

Reports in *Immanuel's Witness* reveal that income for the Children's Home did not always match expenditure, and shortfalls had to be made good from the general funds of the mission. The food may well have been unappetising but, for all that, the children appeared to thrive. Regular medical inspections took place and the children all seemed to be in good health. The Medical Superintendent reported in 1915, "We look forward to our visit each week, because never before have we seen a Home conducted on such lines. It is a HOME and not an Institution. No happier and better cared for children can be found than those at Naomi House. A visit there is a tonic for depressed spirits. The children are so clean, and happy, intelligent and affectionate, that no misanthrope could withstand them. The future of these children is full of promise, as they grow up to know the Lord Jesus as their personal Saviour."

Christmas was a special time at Naomi. The children received gifts, and the great delight for all was the lighting of the candles on the tree on 25th December. A "Lady Visitor" described her visit to Naomi on Christmas Day 1918. It is the only report in which Ernest is mentioned by name, and it appears that from an early age he was endowed with a gift that would come to the fore in later life.

No woman, unless her heart be made of stone, could fail to be flattered when Baby John climbs into her lap. He is simply adorable such a round little face, such plump little arms, such purposeful little legs, and such a kissable little mouth. The treasures he had received at Christmas were still filling his cup of joy to the full — "a wollygog an' a sojer, an' a big ball." He showed them all to me with great pride.

We were in the fine big play-room at Naomi House, Upper Tooting, a Christian Home for Jewish Boys and Girls, and we were surrounded by the happy family which is mothered by one of the kindest and wisest matrons who ever had charge of a home full of children.

Ernest, who used to be the baby and has now attained the advanced age of six, brought along a toy cart on wheels, and in it Baby John solemnly deposited "the wollygog an' the sojer." Toddling across the room he fetched another favourite, "Bunny," to add to the company.

"Would you like to hear them sing?" asked Matron.

Of course I said that I would. In a minute the children had collected and were standing in a little group, with the very tiny folk in front (all except Baby John who had come back into my lap and this time with a toy engine). The boys and girls sang very sweetly, keeping perfect time, and saying their words so clearly.

"How beautiful upon the mountains" came first, and then we had one or two hymns, and some splendid recitations from two little girls and from Ernest, who is not without dramatic gifts.

Parents were allowed to visit their children on Sunday afternoon, and for months the statuesque Italian Jewess arrived without fail. Then suddenly, and without warning, her visits ceased, and Ernest never saw her again. More than eighty years later, he still does not know what became of her. To the six year old, the emotional impact of the abrupt, unexplained disappearance of his mother was a bereavement and horrific nightmares followed in the wake of his loss. Often in the night he was found wandering the corridors of Naomi sobbing inconsolably.

He was not alone in his unhappiness. In spite of the cheerful appearances put on for the benefit of Naomi's visitors, to some degree all the children were emotionally disturbed and a number of them wet their beds. In the early twentieth century and under the austere conditions at Naomi, there was little understanding of child psychology. Bed-wetters were "naughty" and had to be punished. They had to wash and mangle their sheets and were put on bread and water for a day. To the children of Naomi, life was unfair. Why couldn't they have their own mothers and fathers and live in nice homes like other children?

Strict discipline had to be maintained, but the matron, Miss Miller, and her sister did their best to make up to the children for their lack of a mother's love. However, when

Miss Miller left Naomi the disciplinary inclinations of those who succeeded her were not tempered by the same maternal affection. For a misdemeanour he cannot recall, Ernest was once sentenced to stand in the corner of a room from morning to night for a fortnight.

An insight into what the children were like and how they adjusted to life in Naomi is provided by the Lady Superintendent of the home. Writing in 1920, she observed:

> While some of the children, when first received, are very ignorant in regard to Jewish thought and customs, others are "little Pharisees" in their zeal for the traditions of the elders and the practices of their ancestors. For instance, one member of a family of little ones, recently admitted, was very decided when brought face to face with Christian teaching: he would be a Jew all his life, and would die a Jew, most certainly! Apparently, the words were such as he had heard from some zealot. One evening, when prayers were announced, this child left the room, to procure his cap: no Jew would pray with head uncovered! We explained to him that, according to Christian practice, boys as well as men should remain uncovered during acts of worship. He soon fell into line with the rest of the household, it thus appearing that his Judaism was a very superficial affair.
>
> From time to time this lad made anxious inquiry in regard to the food provided. He had been taught to distinguish between clean and unclean, and so he asked whether there was lard in this or that article of diet! On being assured that all was right, Joseph quietly addressed himself to the things provided, asking less questions on the score of conscience or prejudice. With his sisters and brothers he scanned the picture books

supplied in the play-room, and he soon found out more about Christ than he knew before. And to say that the Gospel story struck their imagination, and, in fact, won the admiration, is to speak mildly of the sensations which the words and actions of the little ones so clearly displayed.

To explain. With one of his sisters, Joseph examined a picture-book setting forth the story of Christ. At length they came upon an illustration of the Saviour on the Cross. Said one: "See they crucified Him!" "How cruel!" replied the other; and feelings of pain were expressed in their faces. After the story of the Life laid down, came that of Resurrection victory. Said Joseph: "Look, He came to life again!" Never before had such a thought entered their youthful minds. After all, the One crucified was alive for evermore! In a moment the little ones seemed to realise the Christian position; and shortly afterward the girl asked why she could not be baptized forthwith, so as to become a follower of Christ; and her brother lost no time, but readily expressed a like desire.

Clearly, the little ones were being drawn toward the triumphant Saviour. If He was alive, they were for choosing Him as their Lord! Of course, we told them that they must learn of Christ before setting out on His service. If they would, first of all, apply themselves to the Gospel message, they would, in due time, hear the call of God to become disciples of His Son; and then would come the time for them, even as for others in the Home, to make response in a joyous submission to the sacred rite of Baptism.

We have a two-fold joy in the work among the little ones. First, they are learning the Christian way, under precept and example inspired by devotion to Christ; and secondly, they are commanding, in an ever deeper degree, the prayerful interest of friends of the Mission. This latter fact is relieving us in growing measure of anxiety in regard to the continuance of this important branch of the work.

Two inmates, who for eight years had the joy, the discipline and instruction of the Home, made a public confession of their faith in Christ Jesus, being received into the visible Church, by Baptism, in May last, at St. Paul's, Onslow Square, the Service being conducted by the President of the Mission.

A former inmate has come under peculiar trial in the course of the year. Having been in the Home for six years, and endeared herself to all by her consistent Christian walk, we found for her a situation in a Christian family, where she has given every satisfaction for two years and upwards. Now, at length, the Jewish relatives have determined to undo all that has been wrought in her heart. In the hope of weaning her from Christ and the influence of His people, they have beset her with tempting promises; but we rejoice to say that their efforts have so far been futile. Grace has been given to this young believer to withstand all assaults, and to bear a faithful testimony to her Lord. She is not yet eighteen, and we invoke the prayers of friends that she may be sustained to the end.

The Barbican's director, Christlieb Lipshytz, was an uncompromising evangelical Christian, but he was determined that the children would never forget they were Jewish. On Sundays the children attended the services at the nearby Reformed Episcopal Church, but each week Lipshytz visited the home to teach the children about Jewish history and culture and would read from the *Siddur*, the Jewish Prayer Book. Ernest's memory of church attendance in those days is disagreeable. The services were deadly dull, but worse than that, the children felt they were a fairground attraction. They were "the Jewish children". Lipshytz objected strongly to the children being treated as curiosities and did all he could to prevent them from feeling they were on exhibition.

Though life at Naomi was far from easy and church attendance was less than pleasant, at day school life was frequently intolerable. The children were conspicuously different. They were "Jews", "Christ-killers" and "sheenies". They were taunted and frequently stoned. In the shelter of the children's home, Ernest had imagined that everyone in the world outside was a Christian; at school he was shocked to find himself the object of palpable hatred.

In this sociological crucible, where kindness and severity, love and austerity, overweening affection and ugly anti-Semitism mixed, the character of a Jewish child who would in later years serve Christ in many nations was formed. Who could have imagined at this time that a timid and melancholic boy called Ernest would one day be an instrument of blessing to Jews and gentiles throughout the world?

2
The Juniper

The law was our schoolmaster to
bring us unto Christ. (Galatians 3:24)

During the First World War, British foreign policy became gradually committed to the idea of establishing a Jewish home in what was then Palestine. Following discussions in the British Cabinet, and after consultation with Zionist leaders, the Foreign Secretary, Arthur James Lord Balfour, made the decision known in the form of a letter to Lord Rothschild on 2nd November 1917. The letter, which became known as the Balfour Declaration, represents the first political recognition of Zionist aims by a great world power.

Dear Lord Rothschild,

I have much pleasure in conveying to you, on behalf of His Majesty's Government, the following declaration of sympathy with Jewish Zionist aspirations which has been submitted to, and approved by, the Cabinet.

"His Majesty's Government view with favour the establishment in Palestine of a national home for the

Jewish people, and will use their best endeavours to facilitate the achievement of this object, it being clearly understood that nothing shall be done which may prejudice the civil and religious rights of existing non-Jewish communities in Palestine, or the rights and political status enjoyed by Jews in any other country."

I should be grateful if you would bring this declaration to the knowledge of the Zionist Federation.

Yours sincerely,

Arthur James Balfour

Britain's Prime Minister at that time was David Lloyd George. From his childhood in the Welsh valleys, Lloyd George had been familiar with the Bible. According to him, the Balfour Declaration "was undoubtedly inspired by natural sympathy, admiration and also by the fact that, as you must remember, we had been trained even more in Hebrew history than in the history of our own country. I could tell you all the kings of Israel. But I doubt whether I could have named half a dozen of the kings of England!"

Another member of the cabinet, also steeped in the Bible, was the South African Jan Christian Smuts. He later wrote in his personal memoirs, "The people of South Africa have been brought up almost entirely on Jewish tradition. The Old Testament has been the very marrow of Dutch culture here in South Africa." He had been brought up to believe that "the day will come when the words of the prophets will become true, and Israel will return to its own land."

Balfour had grown up in Scots Presbyterianism, a system in direct spiritual descent from seventeenth century Puritanism. Whatever other influences of his Presbyterian upbringing remained, it had produced in him a profound respect for the Jewish people. He believed "the genius innate in that dispersed people could turn them into a productive nation in their original land". Asked why the Jews should be so privileged, he replied, "The Jew is unique. For them race, religion and country are inter-related as they are in the case of no other religion and no other country on earth."

Ernest Lloyd was four years old when the Balfour Declaration was signed. If concern for the Jews found expression in the British cabinet, in society at large the Jewish people were viewed less favourably. In the economically depressed years following the First World War "the Jews" were seen as the cause of the nation's ills. As unemployment figures rocketed, it became part of urban mythology that while "British" men were fighting the Germans, "the Jews" were at home making money.

Throughout Ernest's childhood, anti-Jewish feeling was an ever-present feature of life. Many of the Naomi children were conspicuously Jewish, and in the streets they were sneered at and taunted as "Christ-killers" and "sheenies". Leo Rosten, in the *Joys of Yiddish*, suggests the epithet "sheeny" may be derived from the Yiddish *schön*, meaning pretty or beautiful, the word German Jewish merchants used to describe their wares. Another possibility is that "sheeny" derived from another Yiddish term, *a miesse meshina*, meaning a terrible fate or death. Whatever the etymology, by the early twentieth century it had become English slang for a tramp or pawnbroker, a low-life or a fraud and therefore, when applied to Jews, a term of utter contempt.

The awareness that they were alone in a world hostile to Jewish people, without father or mother, created in the Naomi children a spirit of solidarity. They had each other. Naomi was their family and they had to stick together. Ernest was very timid, and the older members of the Naomi family shielded him at times when they were under attack from other children. But they were to discover that not everyone outside the walls of Naomi despised the Jews. An elderly lady once defended them from a group of schoolchildren who were taunting them and throwing stones. Gathering the children around her, she told them that her greatest friend was a Jew. Up to this time the children had never encountered a gentile outside Naomi who had showed them genuine affection and they were curious to know about her "friend". She told them that he was Jesus and for that reason she had protected them from harm.

In the years to come, Ernest was to discover to his cost that if anti-Semitism was dangerous, philo-Semitism could be suffocating. Supporters of Naomi visited the home on Sundays and the children were made to wash and scrub their faces until they shone; they had to put on their finest second-hand clothes and be on their best behaviour. The children sang sweetly on demand, but they resented every minute of Sunday afternoon when they became "the Jewish children".

Whatever the shortcomings of Naomi, it was a home where, says Ernest, "the Saviour was honoured". The children were taught Christian truth and many of them believed in Jesus. Nevertheless, they were not coerced into faith. The Naomi Home stood as a refutation of the allegation, as common today as it was then, that Christian missionaries prey on the vulnerable, the young, the elderly, the lonely and the infirm, and that Jews become Christians through psychological manipulation. No child was compelled into the Faith or baptised against their will, and each week the children were reminded of their people's history and religion by Rev. Lipshytz.

A number of the Naomi family went on to serve the Lord as ministers and missionaries. The diminutive and individualistic Kitty Mandell became a nurse and served with the British Jews Society at the Gilead Medical Mission in Fournier Street. The fiery Katie Cutler served for almost forty years as a missionary with the Bible Churchman's Missionary Society in Burma. Mildred Angel worked for many years as a nurse with the Edinburgh Medical Mission in Nazareth, while Rosemary Marshall served most of her life in the Far East with the Sudan Interior Mission and the Overseas Missionary Fellowship. Rose Silverman came from a religiously observant Jewish family, and though she did not enter full-time missionary service, her love for Jesus motivated her to become a nurse. Joseph, Rae and Esther Cohen all entered Christian service. Joseph became a doctor in Rhodesia, Rae and her husband Peter Cody worked with the YMCA, while Esther and her husband Cecil Eman served with the Barbican Mission in Prague, Czechoslovakia.

A later generation of children would also go on to serve the Messiah. Almost twenty years after Ernest entered Naomi, Joseph Schneider and his brother Peter were brought from Czechoslovakia by I.E. Davidson, the then director of the Barbican Mission. Peter entered the ministry of the Anglican Church, eventually attaining the office of canon at St George's Cathedral in Jerusalem. His deep involvement in Jewish-Christian relationships resulted in him becoming a passionate advocate of dialogue rather than mission. Joseph changed his name to Taylor and became a missionary doctor in East Africa. Unlike his brother, Joe Taylor never lost his evangelical zeal and was a very fine missionary. One of his daughters married Jonathan Levinson, son of Stephen Levinson, a later director of the mission. Stephen Levinson was himself a Naomi boy who, with his wife Rosina, served as a missionary in Tunisia before being appointed director of the Barbican Mission to the Jews and ultimately joint director of Christian Witness to Israel.

In Ernest's day, Naomi boys were transferred to Gorringe Park House in Mitcham at the age of thirteen. There Ernest came under the care and influence of the well-loved Hebrew Christian, Mark Kagan. Like Lipshytz, Kagan wanted the boys not only to love the Jewish Messiah but also to remember that they themselves were Jewish. He and Lipshytz were members of the British Hebrew Christian Alliance, and in 1917, at the invitation of Lipshytz, Kagan and his wife became House Father and Mother at Gorringe Park.

The energetic and cheerful Kagan originated from Russia and spoke with a slight accent. Unlike Lipshytz, he was diminutive and dapper and was never seen without a three-piece suit and spats. The boys loved him and they were his "Junipers" (Jew nippers). Each morning the boys would be sent off to school with the admonition, "Mind how you Junipers go".

Kagan had been an Anglican, but in his thirties he joined the Brethren and remained in the Christian Assemblies for almost seventy years. He was a gifted speaker who, because of his insights into the Old Testament, was still in demand after his hundredth birthday, having preached at his own centenary celebration. Kagan was proud of his Jewishness almost to the point of obsession, and was insistent that the staff at Gorringe Park were Jewish. He once stopped a non-Jewish congregation in the middle of the hymn *All hail the power of Jesus' name*, to remind them that they were the "Gentile *sinners*" not the "seed of Israel's *chosen race*".

In his early teens Ernest developed an intense interest in the Old Testament, particularly the five books of Moses. The history of his people, revealed in the Torah, fascinated him, and he became absorbed by the book of Leviticus. The Hebrew title *Vayikra* is taken from the opening words, "And He called...", and throughout the 26 chapters the phrase

"Now the LORD spoke to Moses…" occurs more than thirty times. Ernest had been taught from his earliest days that the Bible was divinely inspired, but it was only at this stage in his spiritual pilgrimage that it became forcefully apparent to him that Leviticus was a divinely revealed message. The book had not originated in the mind of Moses, but had come from God through the great leader of Israel. Ernest reasoned that to approach God one needed an invitation and that Moses himself had no authority to issue such a summons; it was God himself that had called the nation. Ernest found himself engrossed with the details of the ceremonial law and the minutiae relating to the sacrifices and offerings, the fasts and feast days; but even at the age of fourteen there appeared to him to be something inadequate about the law.

Around this time, someone appeared who was to have a great influence on Ernest's thinking and his future life. Ernie Jump was in his early twenties and taught the Crusader class at Trinity Road Baptist Chapel (now Trinity Road Chapel). He was the product of an evangelicalism that emphasised not only the importance of the Bible but also Bible knowledge. The great Bible teachers such as G. Campbell Morgan, W. Graham Scroggie and J. Sidlow Baxter preached to large congregations. "Worldliness" – defined in terms of going to the cinema, dancing, smoking and drinking – was frowned on, and Christian young people were exhorted to study the Scriptures, memorise Bible passages and be witnesses for Christ. Ernie Jump was the ideal of the Christian young man: smart, athletic and with an extensive knowledge of the Bible. Trinity Road Baptist Chapel prayed for the children's home, and on Saturday afternoons Ernie would take three or four of the boys, including Ernest, to Wimbledon Common to play football, after which he would treat them to buns and lemonade.

Initially, the Junipers were suspicious. Throughout their childhood they had suffered abuse from outsiders and were patronised at church. Few in the world outside Naomi had been kind to them, but they sensed that Ernie genuinely liked them and grew to trust him as a friend. After football on Wimbledon Common, while the boys chewed their buns and drank their lemonade, Ernie talked to them about the Scriptures. In Ernie Jump, Ernest found a mentor and a soul mate, someone who could answer his many questions about the Bible and the Levitical rituals and sacrifices.

The historic books of Esther, Nehemiah and Ezra excited Ernest, but the prophetic books presented him with difficulties. The prophets' severe denunciations of the nation puzzled him. Why did a nation with such a remarkable history, and a people to whom God so dramatically revealed himself, depart from their Creator? Ernie Jump helped Ernest to understand the biblical teaching about sin and the solution to sin. From Malachi 3:7, Ernest learned that the way back to God was always open: "Return unto me, and I will return unto you."

As Ernest studied and reflected on the Law and the Prophets, the realisation slowly dawned that he was no different from his rebellious ancestors. Years of deprivation, want and alienation had taken their toll on his spirit. Outwardly, there was no trace of resentment. He was a good boy who took pride in his religious observance. However, he began to see that there was a root of bitter resentment toward God in his heart. Life had been hard, but he had overcome the social impediments and was doing very well for himself. What need was there for him to return to the Almighty?

When he reached the New Testament, the epistles to the Romans and the Hebrews impressed him, but he recoiled when he read Romans 3:23: "For all have sinned, and come short of the glory of God." Ernie Jump wisely pointed out that the words were those of a Jew, one of Ernest's own people. The verse became the key to Ernest's understanding of other passages which, until then, had seemed meaningless, such as Romans 5:1: "Therefore being justified by faith, we have peace with God through our Lord Jesus Christ." Like Martin Luther four hundred years previously, an understanding of the doctrine of justification by faith alone was dawning in his heart. Ernest began to see that any relationship with the God of his fathers had to be on God's terms.

Though he cannot remember the precise time, at the age of seventeen Ernest became a Christian. "It wasn't a Damascus Road experience; it wasn't a light from heaven. But when I really did trust the Lord, it was because I knew that there was nothing I could do to save myself; I knew that everything had been done for me. I didn't feel exuberant, but I had a tremendous sense of peace and I knew there was a purpose to my life. I had handed my life over to the Saviour."

Not all Christian influence was as beneficial as that of Ernie Jump, however. An elderly Christian couple who visited the home developed an affection for Ernest and wanted to adopt him as their own son. At the age of sixteen he went to live with them, but what should have been a very happy situation turned into a living nightmare. Financially, his benefactors were well off, but the couple belonged to the straight-laced, middle-class variety of evangelical Anglicanism that reduced spirituality to a set of rules and regulations. Even to a teenager who had been used to a strict regime from earliest childhood, the claustrophobic legalism of his new surroundings was asphyxiating. If he transgressed, the reproof was swift and sharp: it was the "old Jacob" coming out. The double standard was apparent: his foster parents loved "the dear Jews", but when he displeased them he was reminded that his old "Jewish nature" was raising its less than beautiful head. Ernest began to suspect that behind the sentimental affection they professed for the Jewish people, their motive for fostering him was that they might transform him into a respectable Christian boy, a "trophy of grace" to be put on display. He remained submissive to his foster parents in spite of the misery he experienced, but he cannot recall being happy, even for an hour, while in their home.

Seventy years later, the emotional scars remain, and Ernest still feels uncomfortable and suspicious when Christians profess effusively to love the Jewish people. He believes that most Jewish people feel patronised when Christians assure them that they love Israel and "the Jews". True lovers of Israel speak more eloquently by their actions than by their words. But just as God had his hand on Moses in the palace of Pharaoh, he was also watching over Ernest Lloyd, and in the fulness of time would open a way of escape from the oppressive house of bondage that was his foster home. Ernest's escape, like that of Moses, would be the means by which he would discover the calling of God for his life.

3
Gilead

Is there no balm in Gilead? (Jeremiah 8:22)

In 1933 the Council of the British Society for the Propagation of the Gospel Among the Jews, known commonly as the British Jews Society, was looking for a worker to stimulate interest in Jewish mission among Christian youth. The tall, nervous student sitting before them appeared to be the answer to their prayers. He was young but, more importantly, he was Jewish.

At the time of the interview Ernest was in his third and final year at All Nations College in Upper Norwood, South London. He had enrolled as a student partly to escape the spiritually claustrophobic conditions of his foster home, but more specifically, because he was feeling an increasing constraint to take the gospel to his own people. He recorded in August 1934 that some of the most wonderful days of his life were spent at All Nations. The college was in close proximity to Spurgeon's College and the Missionary Training College. A friendly rivalry existed between the three colleges. They competed against each other in football matches and, on one notable occasion during a midnight raid on Spurgeon's College, Ernest and two friends crowned the statue of the college's revered founder with a chamber pot.

All Nations was also a place where he grew spiritually. In the *Jewish Missionary Herald* of August 1934, he wrote, "When I entered [All Nations], though I had certainly consecrated myself to God, I had not realised the vital part that the Holy Spirit takes in the life of the Christian. It was there that I realised the need of being 'filled with the Spirit'."

Frank Exley, the General Secretary of the British Society for the Propagation of the Gospel among the Jews, was a visiting lecturer at All Nations, and under his influence Ernest felt increasingly drawn to Jewish mission in general and the British Jews Society in particular.

The British Jews Society wanted a young Hebrew Christian to generate support for the work among Christian youth, but the prospect of representing the mission before congregations filled Ernest with dread and he was unwilling to even consider the possibility. As far as Ernest was concerned, he was not a preacher or public speaker, and he expressed his misgivings to the principal of All Nations, H.S. Curr, who was also a member of the society's Panel of Referees. Principal Curr counselled him to pray about the matter, but not to go to the Almighty with conditions. After a considerable internal struggle, Ernest determined that he would do whatever God wanted him to do. If God was calling him to work with the BJS and they wanted him to speak in churches, he would do it.

Following the interview with the Council, Frank Exley called Ernest into his office to lay down some ground rules. The British Jews Society did not make their needs known except to God and it was their policy never to issue public appeals for money. Ernest was in full agreement. His great concern was for the salvation of his people. The Council wanted him to begin in January the following year, but they requested Principal Curr to release him each afternoon of his final term to work at Gilead, one of two medical missions run by the BJS. The other, the Wingate M'Cheyne Medical Mission, was situated in Dean Street, Soho where there was a large Jewish community. The people were poverty stricken, and the now prestigious Dean Street was lined with hovels. Jewish people queued at soup kitchens to receive meagre servings that barely kept body and soul together. There was no National Health Service and many of London's poor depended on Christian Medical Missions to provide treatment. The Wingate M'Cheyne Mission was staffed by Dr Armstrong Harris, assisted by Sister Mary, Sister Elsa and Mrs Lambotte, a former missionary to the Belgian Congo. The mission's evangelist was Bernard Segall, a Romanian Jew seconded to the BJS by the London City Mission. Segall was noted for his eccentricity and had a reputation for not suffering fools gladly. On the eve of his wedding, his fiancée had collapsed and died, and Segall never recovered from the tragedy. His bride-to-be had prepared the marital home in East Finchley, and Segall left everything as she had arranged it. Like the home of Dickens' Miss Havisham, the house remained frozen in time and no one who entered was allowed to touch a thing.

In spite of his personality – or perhaps, in the wisdom of God, because of it – Segall was a first-rate missionary. He ran an excellent Bible study at the Medical Mission, which forty to fifty young Jewish men attended regularly, and Segall had a remarkable ability for being able to turn any situation into an advantage for the gospel. On one occasion he visited a Jewish businessman at his office in Soho in the West End of London. The man was furious and ordered Segall out of his office, calling him a *schnorrer* – a Yiddish term for a good-for-nothing, a scrounger and beggar – and a *meshummad*, a traitor. Segall asked, "Sir, if I can do something you can't do, would you be willing to listen to me?"

"I won't listen to you; you're a *meshummad*!"

"But if I *can* do something you can't do, will you listen to me?"

"All right. It's a deal. If you can do something I can't, I'll listen to what you have to say."

Without hesitation, Segall took out his false teeth, set them on the businessman's desk and invited him to do the same! The man couldn't. "Right", said Segall, "now you have to listen to what I am here to tell you!"

Even more outrageous was Segall's behaviour when a Jewish butcher told him that there was not a word of truth in the Bible. Before the man knew what was happening, the heavy-set Segall had him tight by the nose, wringing it till it bled, and then quoted Proverbs 30:33: "Surely the churning of milk bringeth forth butter, and *the wringing of the nose bringeth forth blood…*" Similar stories of the use of Proverbs 30:33 are in circulation, most of them are probably apocryphal, but Ernest maintains the Segall incident is authentic. Perhaps Segall set an example for others to imitate!

While patients waited to see the doctors at the medical missions, the BJS missionaries engaged them in conversation about their spiritual needs and one of them would deliver a brief gospel talk before the patients saw the doctor. Not all the patients appreciated the broader aim of the mission. They wanted to be treated for their ailments and did not want to hear about Jesus. Jewish women stuffed their ears with cotton wool during the sermon to avoid hearing the name of Jesus. But not all closed their ears to the gospel. Forty years later in Helston, Cornwall, Ernest met Hyman Samuel, a Jewish tailor whose mother took him to the Wingate M'Cheyne Mission when he was a child. Though she sternly instructed him not to listen to "that man speaking", Hymie did listen to Bernard Segall and, as a result, he became a believer in the Messiah.

The Medical Mission to which Ernest was seconded was Gilead, situated on the corner of Fournier Street and Wilkes Street in Spitalfields. Fournier Street ran off Brick Lane, which today lies in the heart of London's Bangladeshi community. Lined with once elegant Georgian terraced houses, the beauty of the area has faded and the brown dust of the narrow street lies thinly but visibly on exterior paintwork. The street signs are in English and Urdu and everywhere the air is tinged with the pungent aroma of Balti and Vindaloo. But in the nineteen thirties, this Asian area was largely Jewish and the Gilead Medical Mission lay in the shadow of Christ Church Spitalfields.

A Jewish dispensary also existed in Fournier Street, but many East End Jews were too poor even to afford the "sixpenny doctors". The missionary doctors had a reputation not only for skill but also for their patience, listening ear and sympathy. The Jewish authorities were bitterly opposed to the medical missions that operated in the Jewish quarters of London, and a correspondent to the Jewish Chronicle in 1923 complained that patients "had first to hear a lengthy sermon preached against our religion, which is held to ridicule, to which they listen in silence, afraid to say a word against the sermon for fear of not being able to see the doctor".

The Gilead Medical Mission made no attempt to hide the fact that it was a Christian mission and surviving photographs show John 14:6 painted boldly on its walls: *Jeshua said: "I am the Way, the Truth and the Life."* The mission took its name from Jeremiah 8:22: "Is there no balm in Gilead?

Is there no physician there? Why is not the health of the daughter of my people recovered?" In the ancient world the fragrance of the balm of Gilead was highly regarded and its curative reputation was legendary, bordering on the miraculous. Balm was extremely valuable, and the caravans that carried Joseph to slavery in Egypt in Genesis 37:25 were loaded with it.

Christians in every age have seen the balm of Gilead as a beautiful Old Testament type of Christ and it inspired the African American spiritual:

There is a balm in Gilead
To make the wounded whole;
There is a balm in Gilead
To heal the sin-sick soul.

Because the Spitalfields mission was established to care for the whole person – body, soul and spirit – Gilead was an appropriate name. Ernest travelled there each afternoon of his final term at All Nations. As a penniless student, most days he walked the six miles to and from Fournier Street. The staff at Gilead were Dr T.G. Churcher (the father of Dr James Churcher, who became a BJS missionary in Haifa), Julia Ridgeway, Nina Banks, Kitty Mandel and missionaries Lewis Newton and B.P. Golowner.

Ernest was twenty when he began working alongside Lewis Newton at Gilead. Newton was a superb missionary; small, self-effacing but completely fearless. He came to Britain from Minsk and never lost his Russian accent. Having come from an Orthodox Jewish family, his knowledge of the Talmud – the colossal collection of rabbinic discussions and sayings that has governed Jewish life and thought for centuries – was immense.

Newton was a patient and kind mentor. He gently eased his protégé into the work. On his first afternoon at Gilead, Newton told Ernest he wanted him to sit with the old ladies and listen to them. Newton talked to the grandmothers and gradually drew Ernest into the conversation: "I wonder what this young man thinks about that…"

Before the patients saw the doctor, there was a short service with hymns, a prayer and a biblical meditation. Lionel Leslie, a Canadian Messianic Jew, came into the world with assistance from Sister Ridgeway and grew up in the vicinity of Gilead. As a child he was taken to the mission whenever he was ill and recalls, that before patients received treatment, they were required to listen to a brief sermon "and a song or two". Many of the elderly patients were immigrants and could speak little English and the children had to translate for them.

Ernest was unhappy with the singing of hymns because it was evident to him that none of the patients knew what they were singing about. A favourite of Lewis Newton was, "When I, the Lord, do see the blood / I will pass over you". However, none but the missionaries understood the terminology. Christians often suppose that Jewish people are deeply familiar with the Scriptures and have an intimate knowledge of the texts. But even such clear allusions to the Passover were lost on the Jewish patients when placed in a Christian context. Eventually Eric Gabe, another of Gilead's missionaries, composed some choruses with Jewish tunes:

When in the synagogue
Our rabbi read the law,
Israel was happy
And Judah praised the Lord.

Gabe's words and music were well received. The Jewish

patients loved the Hebrew words and melodies and would even sing:

> Yeshua, Yeshua,
> Thou shalt call His name Yeshua
> For He shall save His people from their sins ...

When Lewis Newton judged Ernest was ready, he told him that he was to deliver the gospel message to the patients before they saw the doctor. Ernest took as his subject Jeremiah 8:22, "Is there no balm in Gilead?"

> What have you Yiddisher people come here for? Who do you want to see? You want to see the doctor. You have come to see the physician. You are going to see the nurse and you are going to see the dispenser. You are going to get medicine. Why? Because you are not well and it is unpleasant to be unwell. Jeremiah was one of our prophets and he spoke of the sickness of his people. What was the disease he was referring to? And why was there no physician? Some of you have come to see the doctor because you have heart trouble. Now, I can see my hand; I can see my legs; I can see my feet, but I can't see my heart. But if the heart is sick, the whole body is sick...

In ten brief minutes he explained to the patients that they were suffering more than just physically. He diagnosed their spiritual condition and pointed them to the great Physician and the balm for the soul. Following the example of Lewis Newton, after speaking he sat beside an elderly Jewish grandmother with the intention of taking the subject further. Before he could speak, she said, "You shouldn't have changed". He tried to explain that he was still a Jew, but the lady was adamant that he had forsaken his people and was following a gentile religion.

Though most of the patients were happy to sing Hebrew Christian hymns, many resented the compulsory sermon. Those who were inclined to listen to the message feared being seen to be too attentive to the preacher. Others felt obliged to establish their Jewish credentials by openly opposing the Christian message – at times forcibly. A graphic example of the kind of angry responses that accompanied the preaching can be seen in what happened when Ernest was speaking from Deuteronomy 18:18: "I will raise them up a Prophet from among their brethren, like unto thee, and I will put my words in his mouth; and he shall speak unto them all that I shall command Him. And it shall come to pass, that whosoever will not hearken unto my words which he shall speak in my name, I will require it of him." A man suddenly rose angrily from his seat and approached Ernest, threatening him loudly. The young preacher was not intimidated. He calmed the man down and promised to talk to him at the end of the session. At the end of the morning, when the other patients had left, Ernest was able to reason with the subdued heckler and show him the way of salvation.

Working under the fatherly eye of Lewis Newton was an excellent preparation for his future ministry. He experienced first-hand the problems, difficulties and heartaches that missionaries to the Jewish people have to encounter. Face-to-face contact with Gilead's patients was but one facet of the ministry of the mission; there was also door-to-door visiting and open-air preaching.

Most Jewish people in the East End of London lived in blocks of squalid flats, where entire families lived in two room apartments. The abject poverty did little to make them receptive to the Christian message. One of the first encounters

Ernest had after coming to Gilead was with a very old Jewish man. As he looked at the lined features, the young missionary was struck by the look of intense piety in the sharp eyes. The old man wanted to know who Ernest was and why he was calling. Ernest replied that he was a believer in the Messiah and that he hoped to share the Good News of Jesus with him. The eyes darkened as the old bent figure looked up at the young man who towered over him. "Do you know what I think about Jesus?" he hissed. Ernest recoiled in shock as the old man spat at him. He would discover that this kind of reception was not uncommon.

Lewis Newton preached in the open air in the vicinity of the medical mission but made it a principle never to conduct meetings outside a synagogue. Many of those living in Spitalfields were Ashkenazim, of Eastern European origin, and Newton would preach in Yiddish, a language spoken at that time by some eleven million Jews in Russia, Lithuania, Hungary, Poland and the Ukraine. Crowds of Jews would gather to hear, but the Orthodox would heckle, shout abuse and hurl missiles at the preacher. After preaching, Newton would approach two or three people who seemed interested and speak to them, often for well over an hour.

Orthodox Jews were furious at the *meshummads* who dared to proclaim their foreign religion in the heart of London's Jewish community, and were not averse to the use of violence. The fact that Ernest was well above average height did not deter his opponents. The knowledge that Christians are commanded to turn the other cheek may well have emboldened their adversaries, and on at least one occasion, Ernest took a well-placed blow to the face.

But most opposition took the form of verbal abuse and heckling. The Orthodox displayed a bitter hatred of Christ and would shout "*Mamzin! Mamzin!*" (Bastard) directed either at the preacher or as a slur on the person of Christ. In Jewish anti-Christian writings, notably the mediaeval *Toldoth Yeshu*, Jesus is represented as the offspring of an illicit relationship between his mother and a Roman soldier.

Those who were willing to engage in rational discourse had a standard set of objections to the gospel. The New Testament was a *goyishe* (gentile) book and, therefore, not for Jews. Their stock answer to the classic messianic proof text, Isaiah chapter 53, was that the Suffering Servant was the nation of Israel which, at that time, was suffering in Europe under the rising tide of Nazi anti-Semitism. However, though they were vitriolic in their opposition to the street preachers, many of those who shunned the gospel were frequent visitors to the doctor in Fournier Street.

*****

Ernest officially commenced work with the British Jews Society as Missionary Deputation Secretary on 1st January 1934 – three months before his 21st birthday. His brief was to represent the society in churches and to be a missionary wherever he went. The British Jews Society wanted Ernest to stir up interest in their work, but he did not speak publicly on behalf of the mission until the middle of that year. They wanted him first to have experience in missionary work, not only as a preparation for deputation in the churches, but also in order that he might continue to function as a missionary. Many who have seen Ernest in the pulpit would be astonished to know that he dreaded standing before Christian congregations, but he has never been free from the fear of public speaking. There were nights when the prospect of speaking at an important event would keep him awake, and many of those who shared a platform with him would notice a ball of paper being turned over nervously between his fingers while he spoke. Seventy years after Ernest began his ministry, his fingers may still be seen fumbling with his jacket tail even while speaking to a small group of Christian ladies. In years to come, however, his nervousness would do more than deprive him of sleep; it would consign him to a hospital bed.

4

In fear and trembling

I will be with thy mouth, and teach thee
what thou shalt say. (Exodus 4:12)

A service was held to commission Ernest for the work. It was a daunting occasion. He was barely 21 years old, inexperienced, painfully shy and overawed by the dignitaries present. The President of the British Jews Society, Sir Andrew Wingate KCE of the great Wingate family, chaired the meeting and the Rev. J. Chalmers-Lyon of the Presbyterian Church of England, all the more striking in appearance because of his monocle, gave the address.

Prior to Ernest joining the British Jews Society in 1934, the mission had had two full-time workers whose sole responsibility was to represent the society in churches – Rev. Mark Malbert and Rev. Dr Gold-Levin – both of whom had reputations as outstanding public speakers. Malbert had been ordained into the Church of England, but his concern for the salvation of the Jewish people drew him to the BJS, in which he served for many years. The more outstanding of the two was Aaron Philip Gold-Levin, whose brief but colourful life contained enough adventure to fill a novel. Gold-Levin was born the son of an Orthodox Jewish father and an Irish Roman Catholic proselyte in Mariampolis, Russia. A gifted linguist, at the age of three he could read Hebrew fluently and at the age of five he was sent to train as a rabbi. At thirteen he became a convinced Zionist and made the dangerous journey to Palestine alone where, through reading the New Testament, he became a believer in Jesus. Following rejection by his own people and a number of narrow escapes from death, he found his way to London and in 1910 became a missionary with the British Jews Society. He was greatly appreciated as a preacher and as a deputation speaker and became a close friend of Dr Martyn Lloyd-Jones, for whom he spoke at Sandfields Chapel each year.

Ernest stood in awe of his two illustrious predecessors, and when he set out on his first deputation tour in January 1934 he was by no means happy. He toured Cornwall for three and a half weeks, covering almost all the towns and cities of any repute; Truro, Perranwell, St Agnes, Penzance, Marazion, Camborne, Falmouth, Penryn, St Mawes, St. Austell, Newlyn East, Newquay and Redruth. Dr Gold-Levin cast a long shadow. He had toured Cornwall annually for some twenty years and Ernest, whose experience of public speaking up to this time was at open-air meetings or to patients waiting to see the doctor at Gilead, did not relish following in Gold-Levin's footsteps. His fears were confirmed at every step. It was a depressing experience for the sensitive and fearful young man to hear at every church and fellowship how wonderful Dr Gold-Levin was. Nevertheless, the experience was also character forming. Each day Ernest cast himself on the mercy of God and determined that, however great Gold-Levin was, he had to be himself.

Frank Exley, who Ernest viewed as his spiritual father,

had imparted some wise advice based on his own experience of twenty years preaching. He counselled him, first of all, to base all he said in his meetings on the Word of God, and to make his appeal on behalf of Jewish mission from the Scriptures. Exley impressed on him that no amount of enthusiasm and eloquence could make up for the lack of a firm scriptural foundation for what he had to say. Secondly, Exley told him, "Although you're in Jewish work and although you'll be pleading the interests of the British Jews Society, never forget that you may have in your audience somebody who has not touched the hem of the garment of Christ." Although Ernest would be emphasising the spiritual need of the Jewish people, Exley cautioned him never to forget that the gospel was for the gentile as much as it was for the Jew.

Knowing the number of meetings that lay before Ernest that year, he encouraged him not to be over-concerned about preaching the same message in different places. He was bound to repeat himself but, said Exley, what was old material to Ernest would be new to his congregations. "Always pray that the fresh oil of the Holy Spirit may come on old material so that you have that freshness of the Spirit of God in your message." Exley counselled him.

Exley also taught him to respect the views of others. Though a convinced Baptist, when representing the British Jews Society, Exley was non-denominational and shunned controversial subjects. His advice to his young protégé was likewise to stay clear of secondary issues. Listening to Ernest seventy years on, it is abundantly evident that he learned these lessons well.

In spite of his fears, and unbeknown to himself, Ernest was making an impression on the congregations in the South West. At the BJS office, Frank Exley was daily receiving enthusiastic letters from the auxiliary secretaries expressing their delight at the new deputation speaker. The work Ernest had so greatly feared was the one for which he would be long remembered and in which he would be occupied for the best part of his life. Throughout 1934 he travelled the length and breadth of England preaching and setting before churches the spiritual need of the Jewish people.

His report in the March 1934 edition of the mission's magazine, the first of many over the next thirty years, began: "In the recent tour of Cornwall one has been privileged to see real and deep interest aroused in the work of the Society, and to find many whose love for Israel is burning brightly. One of the most encouraging phases of the work has been the number of young people who have attended the meetings, and who, judging from their questions, seemed truly interested in the work."

After his addresses, meetings would frequently be opened for questions. It was an experience he disliked, because questions about eschatology and the future of the Jewish nation occurred with monotonous regularity. He had firm views on biblical prophecy, but whenever he was asked in public meetings if he thought the temple would soon be rebuilt, his stock reply was that the question had nothing to do with Jewish evangelism and was therefore irrelevant. He wanted questions that related to the subject he had addressed.

Jewish missions have acquired a reputation for being associated with an interest in deep, esoteric prophetic speculation. Ernest never regarded prophecy as unimportant and for several years he served on the board of the Advent Testimony Movement, which later became the Prophetic Witness Movement. However, when he spoke as a representative of the British Jews Society, his sole object was to generate a concern for the alleviation of Israel's perilous spiritual condition.

Ernest was not averse to speaking about the Second Advent, but he was unable to divorce the doctrine from the practical imperative to reach Jewish people for Jesus. Miss Victoria Peachey recalls hearing Ernest at his first visit to Quenchwell Chapel in Cornwall in January 1945, when she and two other non-chapel members attended the meeting. Miss Peachey had been persuaded to go, but went very reluctantly. As she entered the hall, Miss Peachey was aware of being in a remarkable atmosphere. The first hymn, *Sing we the King who is coming to reign*, was unknown to her, but the words made a deep impression. She found her attention riveted as Ernest spoke about his work among the Jewish people and their great spiritual need. As he concluded his talk with the words of the Lord Jesus in the book of Revelation, "Surely I come quickly!" she felt that he was challenging her to be able to respond, "Amen! Even so, come Lord Jesus." At the end of the meeting Miss Peachey and her two friends had been born of the Spirit. They became chapel members and supported the work of the British Jews Society from that time on.

The school of prophetic interpretation to which Ernest is closest is classical pre-millennialism, but he has never been a slave to a system. He labels as "diabolical" any school of eschatology that teaches there are different ways of salvation for Jews and gentiles. Though he believes there may be a great spiritual awakening among the Jewish people before Christ returns, he repudiates the notion that Israel will be saved after the rapture or by the sight of Christ appearing in glory above Jerusalem.

Neither does Ernest subscribe to a "Replacement Theology", which views the Church as the "new Israel", inheriting all national Israel's privileges and sees, therefore, no future for national Israel. Chapters 9, 10 and 11 of Romans are seminal to his thinking in this area. He sees those chapters, particularly the eleventh, as a refutation not only of the hypothesis of a second chance for the Jewish people, but also of the notion that God has finished with Israel as a nation. Paul's Olive Tree analogy corrects both errors. There is one Olive Tree, not two. God has not uprooted Israel and planted another Olive Tree in her place, and Israel's hope of salvation lies in Jews being grafted back on to their own Olive Tree by faith in their Messiah.

After the rebirth of the state of Israel in 1948, Ernest was frequently asked whether all the Jews had gone back to their ancient homeland. His answer was that the majority of Jewish people still lived outside the borders of the state of Israel. There were still more Jews in New York alone than in the whole of Israel, Johannesburg in South Africa was commonly known as "Jewburg", Melbourne in Australia had a Jewish population of between sixty and seventy thousand Jews, and the South American nations of Argentina and Brazil had hundreds of thousands of Jewish citizens. Ernest was never content simply to present demographic statistics; he wanted to keep Jewish mission before his audiences. Therefore, because there were Jews in every nation, the Jewish mission field was not limited to one country; it was a worldwide mission. And in case the lesson had not hit home, he reminded his hearers that "our blessed Lord and Saviour did not die for countries; he died for people. It's people that matter to our mission. It's Jewish people that matter, it's Jewish souls."

At times the questions he was asked bordered on the naïve. He was sometimes asked, "If I send a New Testament to a Jew, will he become a Christian?" Jewish mission was far from being that simple. He had been in Jewish homes where a New Testament had been received from an anonymous source. Such well-meaning but misguided attempts at evangelism served only to entrench Jews in their hostility to the gospel.

His standard advice to those who wanted to know the best way to witness to Jewish people was to first of all ask questions. A good initial approach would be to say, "I know very little about the Jewish faith, what do you do when you celebrate the Passover?" Most people respond positively to interest shown in their beliefs, and Jews will readily explain the formalities of *Pesach*. The question can then be taken further: "Do Jewish people still kill a lamb at Passover?" "Why do they no longer observe the ritual?" The answers can then open up the way for further questions that bring Jewish people face to face with their spiritual dilemma and prepare the way for sharing the good news about Messiah as the true Passover lamb. Above all, he believes that it is important to listen. There is a Jewish saying that where there are two Jews there will be three opinions; when attempting to share the gospel with Jewish people, it is important not to assume anything about them. Every Jew is different and to sensitively bear witness requires patience and a willingness to find out where they are coming from.

*****

Ernest tells the story of a little boy who was asked what he wanted to be when he grew up. His parents regularly entertained Christian workers, and he wanted to be a missionary because missionaries always get cakes for tea! Some Christians have romantic notions of what it must be like to be a travelling preacher, but being away from home for weeks at a stretch and sleeping in a different bed every night is far from idyllic. Today, most homes are warm, the beds are comfy and the food is good, but forty years ago deputation speakers could never be sure of the quality of hospitality they would enjoy from day to day.

Ernest's annual tour of Cornwall was always at the beginning of the year, when the weather was often wet and bitterly cold. One January night, he found himself in a damp, cold bed. Unable to endure the cold he got dressed and spent the night in a chair. But the dank conditions had done their work. The following Sunday he preached three times, but felt desperately ill and took the night train back to London, a twelve hour journey in a non-sleeper. He had pleurisy, a serious inflammation of the lungs, and was in bed for nearly three weeks, receiving injections twice daily until his chest cleared.

Having to stay in a different home every few days was never easy but, at the start of his deputation career, he determined never to take people's hospitality for granted. He deplored the tendency of some Christian workers to see supporters and helpers as mere cogs in the mission machinery. Ernest was always a "people person", and his attitude towards supporters stemmed not primarily from the received wisdom passed on by Frank Exley or others but, instead, from a genuine sense of gratitude to those whose hospitality he enjoyed. He treated the people with whom he stayed as personal friends, because he believed they shared his deep love for the Jewish people and his desire for their salvation. His association with the Etherton family goes back to his earliest days as Missionary Deputation Secretary, when he regularly stayed in the family home. On his first visit, Jennifer's mother had bought pork for the evening meal. Realising that a Jew was eating with them, she suddenly panicked and rushed back to the butcher to buy different meat! She needn't have bothered; pork was no problem to

Ernest. He had learned not to call unclean what God had declared clean! The family found it difficult to arrange meetings for Ernest in the Gloucester area, but the family association with Ernest and the mission continued after Jennifer married Peter and moved to Surrey. She remembers:

> Over the years he has spoken in our home, in our church and has shared a few times the Passover meal so powerfully and movingly.
>
> We loved it when Mr Lloyd stayed with us. We felt we were gathering up priceless pearls as he conversed with us, pearls of wealth of knowledge of the Scriptures, pearls of wisdom, pearls of life's experiences from all his travels.
>
> His sense of humour will always remain part of fond memories over the years. His Jewish and Irish jokes would have us creasing up and his own great laugh would just make us laugh too. Peter's memory is of Mr Lloyd totally enveloping a swivel chair we have, which almost took him "head over backwards" on one occasion. Also, whenever he took him a cup of tea in the morning expecting to waken him, he was without fail already sitting up in bed reading the Word and spending time with the Lord he loves so much. What an example of a disciplined Christian life.
>
> His visits would be preceded by numerous letters – often coming from his well worn, well-travelled typewriter which didn't have a spell check! It wasn't that Mr Lloyd couldn't spell, but more like his fingers missed the correct keys on his travels! Likewise after his visits, further letters would follow to "My dear Peter and Jennifer..." thanking us for whatever. Mr Lloyd had an amazing ability to remember family names, friends and always asked after them, how they were

doing – a man so full of love, care and compassion for others and always the perfect gentleman, even when guffawing with laughter.

In Brisbane, Australia, he found himself in the home of a couple of young newly-weds. He could see that they were nervous of the great personage in their home and were very ill at ease. On the second day, after the husband had left for work, Ernest offered to help with the washing up. The young housewife's jaw dropped: "Do *you* wash up?" At the sink they talked, laughed and joked and as the final dish was put away, she said to him, "You know, you're *human*!"

Ernest liked people and people liked him. He endeared himself not only to Christians but also to Jewish people who attended his meetings. Apart from his encyclopaedic knowledge of Scripture and his preaching ability, the two qualities he is most remembered for are his lively sense of humour and his astonishing memory. Lily Gower recalls his visits to Summerstown Mission in Tooting, South London, in the nineteen thirties: "Along with many of the other children, I stood in awe of him. However, when I grew older I came to appreciate his friendliness, his humour, and was amazed at his ability to remember so many people, their names and the churches where he had met them."

Many who were initially angered by his message, warmed to Ernest after meeting him personally. After a church service in the early nineteen sixties, a Jewish woman shook his hand vigorously for about half a minute. She then surprised him by asking if he would go to her home for tea the next day. There was something familiar about the dark-eyed young mother, and he accepted her invitation. The next evening, after tea, she asked if he remembered her. It suddenly came to him that they had met sixteen years previously, when she was seventeen years of age. In his memory he could still see the teenager with eyes full of sadness and anger. She had arrived in England from Germany after losing most of her family in the Nazi death camps.

She asked if he could recall their conversation. He had talked to her about Jesus and she had told him in no uncertain terms that she wanted neither Jesus nor Christianity. She had been venomous and bitter, she recalled, while he had been patient and polite. His final words to her were that if she should ever begin to feel an interest in Jesus, she should buy a New Testament and read it. For four and a half years she had been bewildered and perplexed but she remembered his parting advice. With tears in her eyes, she told him, "Mr Lloyd, it was just as if I was on a stormy sea, and almost shipwrecked, but when I found Christ I came into a harbour of peace".

*****

After little more than a year with the mission, Ernest was billed as the final speaker at the spring meeting of the BJS, and his address was remarkable for a number of reasons. He was barely twenty-two, but his manner of speech showed a maturity of thought and spirituality which, even now, is gripping to read. The style of address, the skill of weaving together personal anecdotes, biblical insights and stories from Jewish sources, combined with personal charisma and passion, would grip and move congregations around the world for another six decades.

Ernest began by telling his audience a story about one of his earliest tours of deputation, some three months after coming into the work. Those were the days of the door-to-door salesman, when travelling hawkers sold household goods out of suitcases. Ernest arrived at an address where he was to stay and rang the bell. A few moments later a lady opened the door. Quickly looking the tall, dark, young stranger over and noticing his bags, she said, "No thank you. I don't want anything this afternoon." After he managed to explain who he was, she was very embarrassed and apologised profusely. She hadn't been expecting someone so young. "I was expecting an old Jew", she explained.

After the laughter subsided, he continued:

Mr. Chairman, I feel the advantage of age this afternoon, after hearing our beloved friend, Dr. Dinsdale Young, a man of ripe age and experience, whom the Lord has used and is using in His Kingdom, and one who has a million times more experience than I have had. But, we thank God that in service for Christ our King age does not matter.

To begin with, I want to tell you the parable of an old Jewish divine, a much revered rabbi to whom the ancient world looked up, a man of very great intellect. It may be a wearisome parable, but it has its meaning. Rabbi Joshua ben Channah, a very plain-looking man, was talking with a princess. "I have often wondered," she said, referring to his extreme plainness, "how so much wisdom manages to hide itself in so common a receptacle."

The sage replied, "I believe your august father preserves his wine in earthen jars."

"That is right," said the princess, "but I don't understand why that is necessary."

"Then tell him to transfer the wine to gold or silver vessels." said the Rabbi.

The princess persuaded her father to do as the rabbi suggested and when the wine turned sour, the king was very angry, and summoned the Rabbi.

"Sire," said ben Channah, "I wanted to give the princess a practical proof that the form of vessels is no criterion for judging the value of their contents."

That is a parable for us to take to heart this afternoon. Jewish missions are a very plain sort of thing. There are no thrills in Jewish work. I wonder sometimes, if I were to say that one of our missionaries had been captured by bandits, whether it would make people sit up. No, there is no glamour in our work. It is a steady plodding. There are no jungles for us to hack our way through; there are no rivers to go down in motor launches, no mountains to climb. It is a very humdrum sort of work but – if one might say so – a very hard work.

Jewish missions are the most unpopular missions in the world, because there is no excitement about them. Our mission work may look very plain on the outside but, as you have heard this afternoon, there is steady progress in it.

Sometimes we sit down after a day's work and think about the people we have met and the various incidents of the day. And I want to review my work this afternoon, as I would sit by the fire and review it in my mind. I am going to think aloud this afternoon.

My work takes me from one corner of England to the other, and I have found that many Christian people are quite ignorant concerning the Jew. Let me read you a letter that I had only a few days ago from one of the largest cities in the West of England. A young lady writes in this way: "I feel that I may not let the opportunity go by without thanking you for the interest that you have roused in me by your meetings, held here in Bristol. Until you visited us at Trinity I had no idea that such a Society was in being and doing such wonderful work amongst the Jews, our neighbours."

That is typical of many, young and old, who, although in the Christian Church, do not realise that the Jew does not have Christ and that the Jew needs Christ. Ignorance prevails. People do not know the slightest thing about the religion of the Jew. The other day a man came into my meeting and, coming up to me, said, "Are you the Jew?"

"Yes," I replied, "I am the Jew, and I have to speak here tonight."

"Well, I am your Chairman, but I don't know what I am going to speak about. I know nothing about the Jews."

I had to bite my tongue, for no Christian has the right to say they know *nothing* about the Jews when he has the Scriptures. As I have gone from auxiliary to auxiliary, I have had to combat this ignorance of Christian people about Jewish work. Certainly, it does cause dismay, when one realises that Jewish evangelisation is one of the most important in missionary endeavour.

But passing from that dismal picture, I take you to my delight at their interest. As I have gone round among the auxiliaries, I have found many, many people who have the interest of the Jew at heart. Many of them are doing all they can by their prayers and by other means to win the Jew for the Lord Jesus Christ.

Between my taking up the work and the passing of our late beloved Dr. Gold-Levin, a number of the auxiliaries fell into decline and it has fallen to my lot to try and revive interest in them. It is not an easy work when one goes into a town where one doesn't know anybody, and is set the task of trying to create missionary interest for the Jew. I confess that sometimes after a day's work in visiting people, calling on those who profess and call themselves Christians and yet are quite apathetic as regards the Jew, I have found it discouraging; but interest is awakening.

I have one auxiliary in mind, which had gone down and down. I visited it not long ago, and now I think it is only this week they are having a meeting among themselves to revive interest. The Secretary whom the Lord led me to has set herself to get a hundred subscribers of two shillings and sixpence [12½ pence in today's coinage] each. The last time she wrote she had only eight, but she was not going to be satisfied until she had a hundred.

During this year, at a meeting, a little girl, not much older than ten, came up to me and slipped a half-crown [12½p] into my hand. I wondered where on earth she had got it and, as I went home that night with the half-crown in my pocket, I wondered whether I ought to have taken it. But a letter came from her mother: "Mary last summer collected blackberries, and instead of getting sweets with the money that she sold them for, she saved it for you."

Mary sold those blackberries because she wanted to help some Jew to find the Saviour.

That is what I am meaning this afternoon. There is doubtless indication that young people are beginning to realise that they, too, can help in this very necessary work.

We have today a great challenge from the Jewish world. The Jewish mission field today presents us with great opportunities. There is, for instance, the changed attitude of the Jew.

A few weeks ago, there was a young Jew of very good education at my meeting. He came up to speak to me and was entirely free from any rancour. He said he attended a synagogue in one of our provincial cities.

"Do you mind talking about Christ?" I asked.

"No," he said, "and I don't mind reading the New Testament, because I have one of my own."

And not only in England, but also on the Continent, in Palestine, in America, the attitude towards Jesus is vastly changing among Jewish people.

A great cause for lament among Jewry today is the growing tide of infidelity. During my journeys, I have been able to meet many Jews and, unfortunately, many of those I have met say, "I have no time for God; I have no time for religion."

You can see in this city of London and elsewhere that the Jewish people are throwing off the bondage of their religion, and agnosticism is taking its place. This is another great challenge.

I was talking to a young Zionist, who said, "Do you know what the solution to our Jewish problems is going to be? Zionism!"

"Well," I said, "there are some stormy seas ahead for Zionism. Zionism can satisfy you materially, but what is there to satisfy your soul? 'For what shall it profit a man if he gain the whole world and lose his own soul?' Have you a religion that can satisfy your soul's need?"

"No" he replied. "Zionism can do that."

"Well," I said, "I have found that the Lord Jesus Christ alone can satisfy the heart need of a Jew."

I wonder how many of us here are fully alive to the need of Jewish evangelism. I read a story, which I will pass on to you. Perhaps some of you already know it. An artist painted a very fine picture. It was going to be put in the Academy. The subject of the picture was *A Church in Ruins*. But everybody who saw the picture thought the artist had played a great joke on them. Instead of a church in ruins, there was a most wonderful church, which showed the interior glittering with gold and silver. A friend said to the artist, "Why do you say it is a church in ruins?" He replied, "Look!" and pointed to the missionary box, which had cobwebs and dust covering it. "A church in ruins!"

Beloved friends, there is a message for us in that. The churches that have no concern for the salvation of the Jew are suffering. They are neglecting the command of Christ, and they cannot do so without loss. This is not our word, but is the word of Holy Scripture: "To the Jew first, and also to the gentile."

May I close with one other illustration? A man came up to me only last year, and said, "I do thank God that one of your missionaries visited my home town."

I asked why.

"Well," he said, "I was a church member. I was on the diaconate. I thought I was serving the Lord fully, but your missionary made a great impression on me. I had been leaving out the Jew. After his visit, I got a missionary box and I took the interest of the Jew to heart. It has done wonders for me. Ever since I have given the Jew his place, my business has gone ahead, my own spiritual life has gone ahead."

When is the whole Christian Church going to learn that when the Jew is put first and his claims are recognised, we shall see prosperity and well-being. "Brethren, my heart's desire and prayer to God for Israel is that they might be saved."

The young man who had feared so much representing the mission before Christian congregations, had embarked on a ministry that would last for seventy years. It was also a calling that would lead him to someone who would be his soulmate for more than half a century.

5
The Key in the Door

Wilt thou go with this man? (Genesis 24:58)

In June 1935, the British Jews Society sent Ernest to Tyneside for a series of meetings that would change his life. He was 22 years old and had no thoughts of marriage. It was not that he was afraid of the opposite sex. He had grown up with girls at Naomi and enjoyed their company. Some of those Jewish girls were vivacious and beautiful, and many of them remained lifelong friends. But Ernest's mind was focused entirely on the work he believed God had called him to do.

Standing under the station clock at Newcastle Central on Friday afternoon, he was approached by a short, dark, prim young woman who asked if he was Mr Ernest Lloyd. She was Jessie McGowan, and he was to stay the weekend with her and her mother and sisters at "Thorncroft", the family home in the leafy suburban village of Stocksfield, fifteen miles west of Newcastle.

Stocksfield lay on the south bank of the River Tyne, well situated for walking in the Northumberland hills. With a population of less than 2,000, it was quiet and peaceful.

"Thorncroft" was pleasant and comfortable without being luxurious, and Jessie was the local secretary for the British Jews Society. She had organised a full itinerary for the weekend, starting that evening, and Ernest had meetings throughout the weekend at a number of churches in the Newcastle area, including Presbyterian, Baptist, Methodist and Brethren.

For the three unattached sisters, the presence in the family home of the tall, dark and handsome Christian worker must have created excitement, and at Sunday lunch Jessie's younger sister asked Ernest if he intended to marry. Was the question offered on Jessie's behalf? Was it to ascertain his eligibility? Had Jessie expressed to her any feelings toward their guest or had she seen the way the shy, young missionary looked at her older sister? Was he aware of the suppressed smiles and knowing glances exchanged between the three sisters? Not wanting to indicate in any way his feelings for Jessie, Ernest gave the sort of spiritual, non-committal answer missionaries were supposed to: "I think that's in the hands of the God who has guided me thus far; if I met somebody I felt that I was being divinely led to – yes".

The subject having been raised, the sisters began to discuss who they would like to marry. Jessie said she "wouldn't mind being married", but thought she would like her husband to be a sailor or someone who would "be away a lot of the time" so she could still have her independence. The hint could hardly have been missed. Jessie may not have openly admitted it, but the attraction between the two was probably mutual and she wanted to find out more about the Hebrew Christian missionary who was staying the weekend.

As the weekend progressed, Ernest and Jessie found they had much in common. Her forthrightness and candour impressed him, and his modesty no doubt intrigued her.

The visit was a success. Ernest was well received at the various fellowships at which he spoke, and on the Tuesday morning Jessie drove him back to Newcastle station. As they stood on the platform waiting for the London train he mustered the courage to ask if she would mind him writing to her. The reply was not quite what he expected: "Have you nothing better to do with your time?"

They began to correspond. Over the months their letters became less formal and in November Jessie invited him to spend Christmas with the family. To the young missionary living on his own in lodgings in Lewisham in South East London, the prospect of spending Christmas with a family – and with Jessie – was irresistible. Rail fares were very cheap, and he eagerly accepted the invitation.

Jessie's letters over the previous six months had revealed nothing of her feelings for him, and over the first few days of his stay he detected no reciprocation of affection. Her apparent nonchalance took its toll on Ernest emotionally, and after Christmas Eve lunch, he excused himself and went out for a walk. Moments later, Jessie followed. She sensed that he was upset. Unable to contain himself, for the first time he expressed his feelings for her. Gently touching his arm, Jessie assured Ernest that she had affection for him also.

Had it been a scene in a Hollywood movie, at this point they would have fallen into each other's arms in a passionate embrace to a background crescendo of strings. But this was Northumberland in the nineteen-thirties and Ernest and Jessie were spiritually-minded, ardent Christians who wanted nothing less than to know God's will for their lives. Nevertheless, it was an emotional moment. "You know," he told her, "I believe you and I are going to go through life together."

"Yes," Jessie said, "I think we might."

Ernest warned her that if she married him, he would be away from home for long periods. She would not be marrying a sailor, but she would be wedded to someone who would have to be away a great deal of the time.

Ernest proposed to Jessie McGowan on 24th December 1935, less than six months after they first met. And she accepted.

Superficially, Ernest and Jessie were like chalk and cheese, but in other crucial ways they were kindred spirits. Ernest was 6ft 2½in tall and Jessie just over five foot. Her long dark hair cascaded down her back when loose and only in her final illness, half a century later, when she was too poorly to care for it, was her hair cut short. Jessie had almost boundless energy and needed little sleep; she possessed an uncommon intelligence and was a shrewd judge of character. After they married, while Ernest slept, Jessie would frequently read and would still be reading when he woke. When she was younger, she had wanted to study for a degree and would probably have gained it with ease had her father not prevented her. But in later years she earned three quarters of her Bachelor of Divinity degree at evening class and later studied Economics. Jessie also attended a teacher training college, but she did not relate well to children; she preferred talking to adults and would have liked to be a lecturer. Another of her thwarted dreams was to pilot an aeroplane, an ambition that was to be fulfilled vicariously years later through their son Peter.

Though her father and mother were Christians, Jessie was nineteen before she came to a definite faith in Christ during a Whitsuntide Conference at which the Faith Mission preacher, Ellis Govan, was the speaker. She didn't agree with all the Faith Mission taught or did, but throughout her life Jessie retained an affection for the society through which she had come to faith. Though she showed her feelings rarely, anti-Semitism infuriated her, and when the mother of a friend expressed her concern that Jessie was marrying "a horrible Jew", Jessie burst into tears.

Like Jessie, Ma McGowan was a typical matter-of-fact Geordie. When Ernest asked permission marry her daughter, her response was a blunt, "That's *your* business."

Ernest had fallen in love with Jessie within an hour of meeting her. Before they reached Stocksfield after she met him at Newcastle Central Station, he knew she was the girl for him. They wanted to get to know each other better, and in the summer of 1936 they spent three weeks in the Lake District, staying in youth hostels for a shilling (five pence in our coinage) per night. Youth Hostels in the 1930s were spartan and strict. There were male and female dormitories and, as Ernest remembers, no "hanky panky was allowed".

On Monday 2nd August 1937, Ernest and Jessie were married at the Methodist chapel in Stocksfield. It was a simple wedding with family and a few friends, including ex-Naomites Rose Silverman, Rae Cohen, Cecil Eman and his wife Esther (née Cohen). Cecil Eman was the best man and Frank Exley, who Ernest viewed as a father, officiated at the ceremony. In his address, Exley shared two principal pieces of advice that Ernest and Jessie sought to follow throughout their lives. Exley counselled them to pray together daily and never to go to sleep with unsettled conflict. During the next half-century, when Ernest was home, not a night would go by when he and Jessie did not read the Bible and pray together.

At the wedding, as ever, Jessie was the non-conformist. She informed Ernest that she was having no fuss. She was not getting married in white. She wanted to be able to wear the frock after they were married and had decided on a green trousseau with matching hat and shoes. Did her husband-to-be object? He told Jessie he was marrying her, not the dress, and that he would go with her choice.

The reception was held in the McGowan garden, after which the newly-weds set off for a three-week honeymoon in the highlands of Scotland. During those three weeks, the couple walked almost 200 miles from Oban on the west coast to Inverness on the east with a 6ft tent, a groundsheet, two blankets and no sleeping bag. Remembering Frank Exley's advice, before setting off each day they read the Scriptures and committed the day to the Lord in prayer.

Returning from their Highland honeymoon, the couple moved into a small rented flat in Muswell Hill, North London. They furnished it with a solid oak sideboard and table with four matching chairs from one of the best furniture shops in London. In all, it cost £15 and Ernest still has the items in his home on the Antrim coast of Northern Ireland.

Muswell Hill Baptist Church, where Frank Exley was a deacon, became their spiritual home for the next 41 years, but Jessie's fiercely independent streak kept her from becoming a member. As a Baptist Church, Muswell Hill required that its members be "baptised believers", that is, baptised by total immersion. Following her conversion, Jessie had been baptised by sprinkling in the Northumberland town of North Shields and she maintained that her sprinkling by a Presbyterian minister was a valid Christian initiation; until she saw the case for baptism by immersion in the Scriptures she would not be re-baptised. More than forty years later, when Jessie was in her sixties, she became persuaded of the Scriptural case for baptism by full immersion and submitted to a second baptism.

The adage that behind every great man there is a good woman was exemplified in the relationship that existed between Ernest and Jessie. He always valued his wife's independent spirit, not least in the advice she offered regarding his public speaking. Throughout their married life, Jessie chauffeured her husband to and from speaking engagements, and as they drove home from his meetings she would often comment on the strengths and weaknesses of his delivery. If she considered that his introduction had been too long, she would advise him to make that part of his talk a little shorter the next time he gave it. If a particular point was not quite relevant or added nothing to the overall argument, she would suggest he omit it in the future. If he had been repetitive, or his line of reasoning had not been sufficiently clear, she would tell him. He always listened and invariably accepted her advice.

Jessie occasionally stood in for Ernest if he was unwell but, like her husband, she was a very reluctant public speaker. She and Ernest were also agreed that Jesus was the primary need of the Jewish people. In the nineteen thirties there was intense fascination among Christians with biblical prophecy, and events in Europe contributed to that interest. As Adolph Hitler's "Final Solution" to the Jewish problem became apparent, Christians wanted to know if the German Führer was the Antichrist. Were the Jewish people about to return to their ancient homeland? Would the temple soon be rebuilt? Was the world on the brink of Armageddon? How near was the return of Christ? Like Ernest, Jessie was willing to answer questions at the end of a meeting, but asking either of them to speculate on matters of prophecy was like waving a red rag to a bull.

Ernest and Jessie had vowed that, whatever the cost, the work to which they had been called by God would have first claim on their lives, and they were to remain faithful to their pledge. They moved into their London flat during the first week of September 1937, attended their first service at

Muswell Hill Baptist on Sunday 5th September, and the following Wednesday Ernest left for a preaching tour that kept him away from his bride until the end of the month. The Lloyds had no telephone, but while he was away Ernest wrote regularly. Each Monday, Jessie received a parcel containing his dirty laundry, which she washed, ironed and forwarded to him.

Frank Exley and his wife took Jessie under their wing and did their best to help her adjust to life in London. But Jessie needed little help; with the use of street maps and guide books, she familiarised herself with London and quickly became adept at finding her way around the capital. Her one handicap was her broad Geordie accent. With increased mobility within the country and the advent of television, regional accents have become more familiar to us all; but in the days prior to the Second World War, few Londoners were familiar with the verbal pronunciations and vocal inflections of the North East.

Jessie was an enigma to many Christians. Her prayer was that she might be "naturally spiritual and spiritually natural", but she could appear abrupt and abrasive. However, behind the apparently unemotional façade beat a tender heart that felt deeply for the less fortunate. She had no patience with a faith without works and would go to any length to help others, whatever the personal cost. In the nineteenth century, evangelicals had had a keen social conscience and Bible-believing Christians had established charities, orphanages and benevolent societies. In the early twentieth century, as theological liberalism and a commitment to the "social gospel" began to spread, evangelical Fundamentalists reacted by emphasising the importance of personal piety. To many Christians, the soul was all that mattered. It would, of course, be inaccurate and churlish to suggest that there was no social concern among evengelicals. Charities, medical missions, soup kitchens and hostels all existed, but it was not until The Evangelical Alliance Relief (Tear) Fund was established in the late sixties that the evangelical world, in the UK at least, recovered a concern for social welfare on a significant scale. In the middle decades of the twentieth century, personal piety was all-important, and spirituality tended to be measured by the number of Christian meetings one attended. To be concerned about social justice and the alleviation of material hardship could mean one's theological credentials were suspect. Ernest's colleague Alan Sax and his wife Frances found to their cost that some evangelicals took a very dim view of those who were willing to get dirt on their hands to share the love of Christ. Alan and Frances were BJS missionaries in Liverpool, and through their ministry three Jewish prostitutes became believers in the Messiah. The ladies had plied their trade at the rear of a large, prestigious evangelical church in Liverpool, and they needed help to begin their new lives. Two of them went to live with Alan and Frances but when it became known that former ladies of the night were living in the Sax home, the leader of the women's fellowship of the church informed Alan that he would no longer be invited to speak to the group. Some of the church ladies had been deeply distressed to discover that a Christian missionary was associating with such persons.

From early in their marriage, Ernest and Jessie were rarely alone in their home. There were always guests, visitors and lodgers; often those who found it difficult to fit in elsewhere. The Lloyd home was always open, and each Sunday upwards of twelve young people who were away from home would enjoy Jessie's hospitality. Even in the war years and beyond, when food was rationed, Jessie managed to feed all that were in need. When she and Ernest were down to a single tin of

"Bully Beef", it was shared with all who were in the house. Sunday visitors were fed and left free to do what they wanted, and to come and go as they wished. The only request was that they attend the Sunday evening Gospel Service at Muswell Hill Baptist Church, but even that was not compulsory. Jessie's philosophy was that it was not enough to simply pray for unsaved people: "I am sick of hearing people pray so piously for souls to be saved without doing anything to help them hear the gospel." Win Hilder, who was a member of Muswell Hill Baptist Church at that time, recalls that a key was always left in the door of the Lloyd home so that anyone could go in and treat it as their home. Ernest and Jessie frequently gave up their bed for visitors, but Jessie insisted that their children should have their own rooms where they could be on their own. That was the rule. Ernest and Jessie would sacrifice their own comfort, but the children were never denied their own space.

Graham Nutman was one of the frequent visitors to the Lloyd residence. He was a lonely teenager but a good soccer player, and when the Muswell Hill Baptist Church football team invited him to play for them he readily accepted, but he refused to attend church. Ernest and Jessie supported the Muswell Hill team and attended the matches, and Graham soon became a regular guest at their home, not only on Sunday afternoons but also throughout the week. His parents had separated and the Lloyd home became a sanctuary of peace and rest for him. At any time he could walk in and feel he was in his own home. When Graham became a Christian his mother was so furious she hurled a vase at him. In spite of his pleas, Mrs Nutman did not want to meet the lady who had influenced her son so much: "If I met this Jessie Lloyd, I'd probably end up a religious idiot like you!" When she finally agreed to meet Jessie, Mrs Nutman was on her guard, but at the end of the evening she told Jessie she liked her. She appreciated not only Jessie's frankness, but also the fact that she had not attempted to force her into a Christian commitment. Graham's mother, too, was eventually converted.

In addition to the comings and goings of their various guests, the Lloyds frequently had people living with them. When the colleague of a nurse who lived with them for nineteen years became homeless, without hesitation Jessie made room for her in the home. The woman in question was a drug addict and the mother of three illegitimate children. She was a troublesome guest, and at two o'clock one morning Ernest and Jessie had to take her to the hospital to have her stomach pumped after she swallowed an entire bottle of aspirin. Some in the church were horrified that Jessie had taken a woman of dubious morality under her wing, especially with two young sons in the house. Nevertheless, Jessie didn't give up; she was prepared to do anything she could to show the love of Christ to those who needed him. Each Christmas Ernest receives a letter from the woman his wife did so much to help. The letters always ends the same: "I'll never forget what Jessie did to make me a Christian."

Another of the unfortunates Jessie helped was a disabled young man who wanted to better himself academically. He had a brilliant mind, but a severe physical deformity made it impossible for him to write. Jessie accompanied him to evening classes and typed his essays and, as a result, he passed his exams with flying colours.

Luton CWI auxiliary secretary Fred Odell recalls Flossie Lewis, who was badly deformed with a hunch back and a club foot, who regularly sent donations for the society through him. When Fred asked why she gave so faithfully to the mission, Flossie told him of the kindness shown to her by

Ernest and Jessie. They had been good friends to her and she had spent many happy holidays with them. "To me," says Fred "it's inconceivable that the Lloyds had any ulterior motive, other than showing Christian compassion to such as Flossie, who would otherwise be passed by."

*****

In September 1939, the whole country was on alert, and Jessie Lloyd was heavy with child. Adolph Hitler had invaded Poland and the whole of Europe was preparing for conflict. Britain's young men were being called up for military duty and London was blacked out. At noon on 3rd September, the British Prime Minister, Neville Chamberlain, declared in the House of Commons, "This country is now at war with Germany. We are ready." Less than thirty-six hours before that momentous declaration, late on 1st September 1939, Jessie Lloyd had a proclamation of her own. She woke up with a start and announced, "I think that whoever's coming is going to come soon". There was no phone in the house, so Ernest had to make his way to the nearest public phone box, only to discover that their doctor was away and all the nurses had been called up. The nearest medical facilities were in Holloway at the BJS Home for Aged Hebrew Christians, which had become an asylum for Jewish refugees from Germany. The matron, Mrs Lambotte, was a fully trained mid-wife but, due to the national emergency, there was no public transport; London had come to a standstill. In pitch darkness Mrs Lambotte walked the three miles from Holloway to Muswell Hill, accompanied by Paul Freed, one of the refugees. In the nineteen thirties there were no pre-natal classes and husbands were expected to keep well out of the way at the birth of children. Nothing had prepared Ernest for this. If standing before a congregation to speak was nerve-racking, this was sheer terror. Mrs Lambotte arrived to find Jessie in the advanced stages of labour and Ernest emotionally distraught.

Mrs Lambotte immediately dismissed Ernest and Paul to the lounge while she attended to the needs of Jessie. The door and walls of the bedroom could not contain Jessie's screams and, as he sat with Paul, Ernest was overcome with fear and despondency. Paul talked in an effort to distract Ernest's thoughts. He was sixteen and had been brought up in an Austrian Jewish home. After Germany annexed Austria in March 1938 and Hermann Goering warned all Jews to leave the country, Paul and his brother were brought to London by the British Jews Society which, with the assistance of the Hebrew Christian Alliance, provided for their welfare. Though most of his family perished in Hitler's death camps, Paul went on to become a professor at Hope University in Holland. He and Ernest remained in contact, and every letter Ernest receives from Paul still says he will never be able to repay the debt that he and his brother owe to the British Jews Society for giving them a new start in life.

At 5.15am silence fell on the apartment. Jessie's screams ceased and Mrs Lambotte emerged smiling to say it was all over; Ernest was the father of a son. Jessie was admitted to a nursing home the next day and, although travel was severely disrupted, Grandma Lloyd managed to get down from Tyneside to be with her daughter and grandson Peter.

*****

With the outbreak of war, Ernest was called up for military service. He completed his papers, but was informed that because he was a full time Christian worker he was in a reserve occupation and would not be required to serve in the armed forces. For the duration of the Second World War, Ernest continued to travel the country pleading the cause of Jewish mission. During just one year – 1942 – his travels took him to 24 English counties, South Wales, Northern Ireland and Eire. He preached 75 times and delivered 230 addresses on behalf of the Society to groups as diverse as Christian Endeavour societies, Sunday Schools, Women's meetings, gatherings of soldiers and airmen and at churches across the entire denominational spectrum.

Absence from home had never been easy for Ernest, but to leave a wife and baby in the capital of England when the country was at war was twice as hard to endure. It was, of course, even harder for Jessie. However, they had made a vow that the Lord and his work would always take precedence, and they were agreed that they could not break it. Their faithfulness to their pact was tested throughout the war years. At the height of the Blitz, a bomb exploded in the road outside their small flat and blew in all the windows. The cot in which Peter was sleeping was covered with glass, but there was not a scratch on him. While Ernest was away on behalf of the BJS and Jessie was alone in the flat with Peter, she suffered a miscarriage. Peter did not come through the hostilities of war unscathed. At a very young age he lost all his hair, a result, the doctor said, of the trauma of the Blitz.

On 7th October 1943, while Ernest was away on a deputation trip, Martin John Lloyd was born. His father did not see him until he was six days old, but his entrance into the world was in more congenial circumstances than those in which Peter was born. Another addition to the family came in 1947 with the arrival of Jennifer, who had been born six years earlier to Jessie's older sister. When her mother died of cancer, the six-year-old Jennifer became a sister to Peter and Martin and lived as a member of the family until her marriage.

*****

A disgraceful aspect of British society in the war years was the survival of anti-Jewish feeling, even in churches. Ernest tells the story of when he boarded a bus one Sunday to go to church and sat next to an elderly lady who carried a Bible under her arm. Ernest was conspicuously Jewish and the lady with the Bible edged as far away from him as she could, gazing contemptuously out of the window. Ernest asked her if she would move away from the Lord Jesus if *he* sat next to her.

In August 1943, Ernest wrote in the BJS *Jewish Missionary Herald*: "If one sometimes has to remove ignorance from Jewish minds one also meets it in dealing with Gentiles. I welcome questions at my meetings, and almost inevitably, I am asked, 'Why are Jews in black-market enterprises?' I try to point out that we cannot deal with the race but only with individuals, and remind my friends that from Jewry came Monotheism, the Torah, the music of the Psalms, and finally our blessed Redeemer Himself. But, whether Jew or Gentile, we are dealing with all humanity, and every man needs the Gospel. One has to try to get people to look upon the Jew not as super-good or super-bad but as a human soul, needing a Saviour, and one over whom the Lord Jesus yearns with compassion and love."

Ignorance of the Jewishness of Christianity was rife in the churches. In April 1948, he wrote: "After I had preached at a large church one Sunday morning a gentleman said to me, 'I have never realised until this morning that Paul was a Jew, and that we owe Christianity to the Jewish nation!'" More astounding was the remark of a man who thought Jews believed in "the same religion" as Christians! After a weeknight meeting, a young lady told him that, as a result of his message, she would go away loving Christ in a far deeper way, and would do all she could to combat the poison of anti-Semitism that was rife in her office.

Ignorance of the spiritual plight of the Jewish people was widespread and expressed itself in opposition to missionary work among the Jews. A businessman who was also a church officer expressed the opinion that missionary work among the Jews was "wasted expenditure and crass impudence". Judaism, he stated, was a great faith and the Jews a great people. Ernest asked him what nationality Paul and the other apostles were, and why Christ had commanded them to preach the gospel to all nations, "beginning at Jerusalem"?

Prior to a visit Ernest made to Penzance in 1941, someone had written to the local newspaper: "Alas, a perusal of some of the objects for whose support we are asked, makes one despair of arousing people to a sense of danger ... we are called to supply capital for the conversion of Jews to Christianity ... turn your forces from this paltry siege and stir them up against a mightier force."

At the same time, there were encouragements. In August 1943, Ernest concluded his report, "In Journeyings Oft…" with the following:

> I feel it to be essential to get young people interested in the Jews and in what we are doing on their behalf, for as youth comes to think in higher terms of Jewry, Jewry will come to receive greater tolerance. Through a hint of mine, some young people visited a local Synagogue to get to know at first hand something of the Jewish outlook and belief… It is always a joy to speak to children in the Sunday school. One little lassie of ten came up to me and said, "Mr. Lloyd, ever since you were here last year I have prayed for Jewish boys and girls, that Jesus will make people kind to them, and kill Hitler"! Another lad of eleven said, "Ever since you were here last I have made friends with a Jew at school, and when others tease him I stick up for him."

May the great Lover of children bless my effort to get them to see Jewry through the eyes of Jesus.

In 1945 Hitler was defeated and the Second World War came to an end. Throughout the hostilities, Ernest had continued to keep the work of the mission before the Christian public at considerable personal cost. As the Lloyds rejoiced with the rest of the country that the dark cloud that had shadowed Europe for more than a decade had passed, neither of them could have guessed that in a few short years Ernest would face the greatest challenge of his life as a missionary.

6
To Boldly Go...

*When he putteth forth his own sheep,
he goeth before them...* (John 10:4)

In 1951 a change occurred in the British Jews Society that
would irrevocably affect the lives of Ernest and Jessie. Their
vow that the Lord and his work would always come first had
been tested continually, especially during the war years. The
pressures on them were great, and they could hardly have
imagined that any greater demands could be made on their
commitment. As the missionary responsible for deputation,
Ernest was away from home for several weeks each year
preaching and speaking on behalf of the society. An example
of a typical year for him is found in a report written for the
August 1947 issue of the BJS magazine. The report reveals
not only his broad range of activities both as deputation
speaker and as a missionary, but also the widely varied nature
of his speaking engagements and the phenomenal number of
them (just eight short of one a day for that year). The account,
entitled "He Goeth Before", is worth reproducing in its
entirety.

Looking back on a year that has been momentous for both Jew and Gentile, and in which I have traversed the British Isles, one remembers the words of the Redeemer in John 10:4. "When He putteth forth His own sheep, He goeth before them." How very true this has been in the course of another year for, despite many difficulties, of sickness, and abnormal travelling conditions, one has realised the unseen, yet ever present reality of the Lord's Presence, and I am grateful to Him for the strength to carry on the work of bringing enlightenment to Christian people, and proclaiming Christ for Israel.

As far as statistics are concerned, one can record the following: my journeyings have been in twenty-five English counties, and visits have been paid to both Eire and Ulster and to South Wales. On behalf of the Society I preached seventy-two sermons and gave 230 addresses at various types of meetings. Altogether, 127 places in Eire and Ulster, England and Wales were visited. One was also glad to get new openings, and so to get the need of the Society's work more widely known.

Contacts With Jews

I should like to record, firstly, contacts made with Jewish people. One can safely say that in Evangelistic effort amongst the Jews, it is, generally speaking, the personal contact that reaches them. Although my work is to seek to secure the interest of Christians in our ministry, I am ever aware of the need of my own Jewish brethren, and am grateful to God for opportunities afforded me for witness to them. May I cite some instances of personal contact?

In a large town in the North I was able to meet a very intellectual Jewish girl, a native of Prague. At first she viewed me with grave suspicion, for her mind was embittered by things she had heard concerning Jewish

Christians. She said to me, "In Prague many Jews were baptized for so much money in order to try and escape Hitler." Her conception of the Christian faith was that all one needed to do was to be baptized. I asked if she really derived satisfaction from Judaism. Her reply was, "One has to strive, for, after all, we can never really know definitely our destiny." We had a long talk, and she promised to read the New Testament. She is in charge of a Refugee Hostel under the care of the Orthodox authorities.

In another county in the West of England I met a most brilliant Jew, who, prior to the Hitlerite tyranny, had been a Professor of Philosophy, but now sells brushes for a livelihood. Over the meal table he quoted extracts from Plato, Socrates, Heine, etc. Everything, he thought, must be reasoned out in the mind. My question to him was, "What is the hope of the Jewish people today?" He shrugged his shoulders, and replied, "Who knows?" I asked him, "What about the Messianic hope of our people?" His answer was, "The Messiah is not a person but a System which man is gradually building up through pain and suffering." I spoke to him of a Saviour Who gives deliverance not from the yoke of Hitlerism or Antisemitism, but from the most enslaving of all things, sin. This good man listened most kindly and patiently, and once more the seed was sown.

I was able to meet a very nice young Jew in the R.A.F. in a small town in the West of England. He is a native of a big city in the North. The tragedy of his position was that he was bordering on Agnosticism. His creed was more or less based on the ethics of Communism. We had a long talk, and among the things I said to him I remarked, "When Israel reared another god, the golden calf, then at once they were in trouble". He at once replied, "I cannot accept the Old Testament, for most of it is hearsay." My answer was that whilst nations and empires had come and gone, and man was ever changing, the Word of truth ever remained. Communism could never satisfy him, only the "Living Water", the truth found in Messiah Jesus, would do that. I was able to let him have a New Testament, and to put him in touch with some very fine young people who may be able to help him.

One of the most interesting of these Jewish contacts was with a young student in Eire. He and his family were Czech Jews, who managed to get out of that country before the Nazis reached there. His father was a most influential man. This young Jew was most friendly, and we had some interesting conversations. I do feel that at heart he is a true disciple of Christ. He has since written me, asking me whether, when I next visit the City where he lives, I will come and visit his father and mother, and other relations. We are corresponding, and I covet most earnestly his parents for Christ, for if they were believers the effect on that Jewish community would be considerable.

Another Jew was most irate in a meeting at which I was speaking. He just could not keep quiet, and once or twice shouted out abuse at me and scorn at what was said. After the meeting I immediately went up and engaged him in conversation. He charged me with being a turncoat, a traitor to the Jewish community. I was now lost to the Jewish people, he said, and he thought all Jewish Christians were a blot on the race, a perfect disgrace. I told him I was not a traitor and, quoting the words of Disraeli, "Half the world worships a Jew, the other half a Jewess". I said, "If Jesus were an American, and all the world except America did Him homage, should we not say that America was stupid and traitorous?" I concluded by telling him that we must as a nation be reconciled to God through Christ, who, after all, was one of our own flesh and blood.

I pass on now to contacts made with non-Jews in trying to enlist support for the Society.

Factory and Business Establishments

On more than one occasion it was my privilege to speak at large works on the Jewish question, taking maybe as a subject "The Jewish riddle: its only answer". These meetings always brought out a great many questions to which, with the aid of the Lord, I was able to give suitable answers. After one such meeting, a young man came up to me, saying that he had been an avowed anti-Semite, but it was, "Simply because I did not know the facts of the case. My whole outlook is changed, and I will strive from now on to counteract the growing evil of Antisemitism". Better still, in these meetings, one was able to present Christ as abundantly able to save both Jew and Gentile. One cannot underestimate the value of these openings.

Rotary Lunches

Here again is a most useful way of enlisting support. One deals with the Jewish problem from an ordinary angle, working up to the spiritual need. At such a meeting are businessmen, sometimes somewhat prejudiced towards Jewry. After one such gathering, a good gentleman said, "I really do not see any need for your work. Both Jew and Gentile are entitled to their own opinions. Let Jew and Christian mix together and pool their mutual resources." I said that there was only one opinion that counted for anything, that which was in accord with the Word of God; that both Jew and Gentile could only approach the Throne of God through the Cross and the work of Calvary. One of its greatest blessings came to the world when Saul of Tarsus saw the light of Christ. We had a very helpful talk, and he said he was most grateful that he had met me.

Young People's Gatherings

How vital it is to capture the attention of the youth of our land, in the interests of Israel. Upon our youth depends whether in the future the lot of Jewry is made easier or harder. I have had at least fifty openings of various types amongst young people throughout the past year. I record a meeting amongst seventy or eighty young people between seventeen and thirty years of age. It was my privilege to go for a hike with them, followed by tea. Afterwards I gave an address and invited questions. The invitation was accepted, and for over an hour I was bombarded with questions which showed what youth is thinking. They were such queries as these: "Where do the Jews get the right to Palestine from?" "Why are they so race-conscious?" "How can an ordinary Gentile Christian get into touch with a Jew?" "Why was Hitler so against the Jews?" "What is the root cause of Antisemitism?" These are but a few of many asked at that particular meeting.

I felt I had not merely made new friends for the Society but for the Jewish people. I have been most impressed by the growing interest amongst young people. It was a great joy to address the students of Trinity College, Dublin, when the room was packed quite full. Once again I invited questions, and found many forthcoming. I was also to meet more than one whose eyes were turned towards the Jewish Missionary field. I may mention a young couple who have a great spiritual yearning for Israel. Many young folk come to their home, and they keep one of our Missionary Boxes in a prominent place. When last opened it contained almost £14. It is so cheering in these days to find that the younger generation are doing now what their parents did in days gone by, entertaining the Jewish Deputation. I think also of the opportunities afforded me of speaking to Sunday Schools. One such memory is of a hall full of children, of the elder boys asking me many questions, and of one boy saying, "Our superintendent has always made us pray for the Jews, that they might become Christians." I have many little friends who in days to come will be, I believe, earnest workers for Israel's salvation. May the Lord raise up many more young people to further our work amongst Israel. I have been able to address Christian Endeavour meetings, Wesley Guilders, Young Life Campaign meetings, Christian Unions in Colleges, these amongst many.

Churches, Chapels, Mission Halls

With humility and gratitude to God I can record that now and again one has reason to believe names have been added to the "Lamb's Book of Life". I may mention a young lady who came right out to the front after an evening meeting, to signify her desire to serve and own allegiance to the Lord Jesus. I hear she is going on well in the Christian life. I think, too, of a young man recently back from India and now demobbed. The lad of many a prayer from Christian parents, he had been "going the pace". He happened to come to an evening service and asked to see me. That night in the vestry I had the great joy of pointing him to the Saviour and of knowing that the angels of God rejoiced over a sinner that repented. He now is making a courageous stand for his Master and Lord. If one sees such as these brought to the foot of Calvary, one not only rejoices with them but is glad that new friends have been gained for the cause of Christ amongst Israel.

*****

The Importance of Being Ernest

William Renshaw Newton was appointed as the General Secretary of the British Jews Society in 1950. He succeeded Arthur G. Parry who, after a long illness, had died on 14th December 1949. Parry had become the General Secretary of the British Jews Society after Frank Exley resigned from the post in 1936. Exley was elderly and felt he could not adequately fulfil his duties. Parry, who was the minister of Carey Baptist Church in Reading, was appointed to the post within three months of Exley's resignation.

Ernest had had a very close and friendly relationship with Frank Exley. They were kindred spirits and Exley had been like a father to him. Ernest's relationship with Parry had not been close, and during Parry's final illness another shadow had hung over the BJS. Ernest had received a very attractive invitation to head up the Canadian branch of the Hebrew Christian Alliance and, at one point, many who knew Ernest felt it was likely that he would accept. However, his primary concern was for the salvation of the Jewish people and, with the coming of Will Newton, Ernest decided to remain with the BJS.

Will Newton had served as a Baptist minister in Cornwall, Devon and Kent and, like Frank Exley before him, he was a gentle and quiet man with a heart for the Jewish people and a concern for the welfare of the missionary staff. He had been converted in 1924 and was baptised in the river Kishon, the scene of Barak's victory over Sisera. Unlike Frank Exley, Will Newton knew little about things Jewish and had met very few Jewish people. However, he was an excellent writer, and supporters of the mission looked forward to his monthly column in the BJS Herald. *From the Secretary's Chair*, his homely editorial, was written as a letter and invariably began, "My dear Friend and Fellow-worker..." The articles were usually based round a verse of Scripture and sprinkled with anecdotes and poetry, references to hymns, popular songs and even nursery rhymes. His column soon became the first thing supporters looked for in the magazine.

Until the Second World War the BJS had concentrated its efforts in the UK, Europe and Israel, but the war brought about the closure of its mission centres on the Continent. Newton settled into the office quickly and addressed the challenge of expanding the work of the BJS to areas where there was no ministry to Jewish people. In April 1950, he suggested to the Council that as Eastern Europe was closed to Jewish mission, the BJS should look to where there were needy communities of Jewish people in other parts of the world. He had in mind primarily South Africa, Canada, New Zealand and Australia. In the 1930s and 40s, South Africa had seen an influx of Jews, precipitated by the persecutions in Europe and the country's rapidly expanding fields of business, so that in 1950 the Jewish population of the country numbered 110,000.

Like Exley, Will Newton quickly became a personal friend to Ernest, and shared with him his vision for expanding the work of the mission. Newton felt Ernest was the man to do the spadework and asked if he would be willing to go to South Africa the following year. Ernest was more than willing, but Newton wanted him to talk the matter over with Jessie and pray it through. The mission had no contacts in any of the places he wanted to plant. It would be pioneer work and Ernest would probably be away for the best part of a year. There was no hesitation on Jessie's part when Ernest spoke to her; the work of God had to come before personal considerations. Jessie might not have married a sailor, but in the next few years her husband was to spend several months at sea. He had to travel as cheaply as possible which, in the years following the War, ruled out flying.

Newton suggested he set off at the end of the following January. The BJS had no contacts in South Africa, so Ernest had to organise his own itinerary. His valedictory service took place on 7th February 1951 at Muswell Hill Baptist Church. Ernest and Jessie's minister, Ronald J. Park, presided over the packed meeting, consisting mainly of church members. Will Newton gave a brief account of "the considerations that had led to the freeing of Mr Lloyd from his ordinary duties", and explained that "Mr Lloyd's journey was the result of deep concern and much prayer for the Jewish people of South Africa. Out of a desire to do everything possible to make known Jesus as Messiah and Saviour to South African Jewry, the prospect was planned and the itinerary worked out." He urged the gathering to pray for Ernest. He was going on behalf of the Society to examine the possibilities of establishing a mission to the Jews of South Africa. His brief was to stimulate an interest in Jewish mission in the churches, to make as complete a survey as possible of the Jewish community in South Africa, and to assess the work already being done. Following Newton's address, Ernest spoke briefly from 1 Corinthians 16:9 and 2 Corinthians 2:12 on "Open Doors of Opportunity".

There are two quotations from the pen of the apostle Paul that form the basis of my thoughts tonight. In the first instance the words are, "For a great door and effectual is opened unto me" and the latter text runs, "Furthermore, when I came to Troas to preach Christ's gospel and a door was opened unto me of the Lord". In looking forward to my visit to South Africa for our Society, I feel that there are these wide open doors of opportunity. In other parts of the mission field doors are closing, as in China. As far as Europe is concerned, our gospel work amongst our Jewish people is practically at a standstill, for our Society has lost its work in Vienna, Krakow, Wilna and Budapest. But if the Lord shuts one door He, in His Sovereignty, opens another, and this is the case regarding South Africa. Our faith in the Lord was honoured, for openings are pouring in daily now. Friends in South Africa are welcoming the visit, and we are most cheered and encouraged by the letters received.

My visit is of a dual nature, and tonight I want first of all to consider the first object of the tour, that is, to witness to the Jewish people. I cite but one example of the opportunity offered. A lady writing from a somewhat remote town near East London tells how she had been talking to a Jewish doctor who said to her, "You send missionaries to the black people to tell them of Jesus; why does nobody preach to us the Christian message?" What an indictment! This good lady said, "A Jewish Christian is coming from England on tour," and immediately this doctor said, "Then we must get him to speak to our Jewish people." I am so cheered to know that I shall have several gatherings of Jews to address whilst out there. I shall also be meeting Hebrew Christians, and the Hebrew Christian Alliance have honoured me by asking me to address their Annual Meeting in Cape Town; this will be a great privilege. I feel that the Lord has a real work to be done through our Society in South Africa.

The second purpose of the tour is to arouse interest among the redeemed people of the Lord in South Africa. Where you have a large community of Jews, you have almost every time the evil of anti-Semitism, and it will be my purpose so to exalt our Lord Jesus that He might be the great antidote to that evil thing. One is so cheered by the letters of welcome already received

[from] many ministers of the gospel throughout the Union, and the meetings are growing in number every day. How grateful we are for the help of dear Miss L. Harris of Cape Town who so willingly is doing all she can to further our work there, to Rev. Glyn Tudor of Durban, and many, many others.

In the course of my tour I shall be spending nearly a week at a Camp with university students, giving a series of talks bearing on the Jewish position; I shall also be speaking at Women's Guilds, and other meetings, all with the express purpose of arousing interest in the taking of the Gospel to Israel. I do wish to make it plain that my visit is *not* to raise money. If I am in the will of the Lord, and our Society tries to do His will, then that part of the visit will be looked after all right. I only ask for the prayers of my fellow church members, and what a joy it will be to go forward knowing that Muswell Hill Baptist Church is behind me. Paul says that although the doors are open, "There are many adversaries." I am aware that it is so still. I shall meet hostility from the Jewish people, ostracism, and bigotry. I may meet the manifestation of anti-Semitism, but the open door is there and I must not be daunted by the Adversary however potent he may be.

*****

Ernest had good reason to be confident of the Lord's blessing on his coming tour. He was still elated after a remarkable experience he and fellow missionary, Julius Katz, had had in Belfast the previous December. The two men were introduced to Mr Cohen, an orthodox Jew whose fifteen year old daughter had accepted Jesus as her Messiah. He and the rest of the family had been deeply distressed by what they perceived to

Above: The earliest picture of Ernest.
Below: The Naomi Home. Ernest is second from the right, front row.

Above: The teenager.
Below: All Nations College, the Class of '33.
Ernest is in the back row, third from left.

Above: Gilead Medical Mission, Fournier Street, Spitalfields.
Below: Jessie and Ernest, the newly weds, 1937.

Above: Jessie with the two boys, Peter (behind) and Martin.
Below: Ernest preaching in East London, South Africa, 1955.

Above: Ernest in the 1950's.
Below: Ernest on Mount Carmel, 1958.

Above: Ernest as Overseas Deputation Secretary, 1959.
Below: Ernest and Jessie on a Scottish holiday, 1964.

Above: David and Goliath. Ernest with Al Preston in South Africa.
Below: Ernest and Jessie with Brian and Vicky Wells
in New Zealand, 1978.

Ernest lecturing at the CWI Summer School, 2002.

be Rebekah's betrayal of her people and had tried every possible way to make her return to Judaism. The rabbi attempted to persuade her that she had been misled and the family threatened to disown her, but Rebekah remained resolute in her faith.

By the time Ernest and Julius were introduced to him, Mr Cohen had had a number of lengthy conversations with a family who attended Great Victoria Street Baptist Church in Belfast, and he had started to read the New Testament. Apart from his daughter, he had never encountered "Hebrew Christians" and considered the term to be self-contradictory. On a Saturday afternoon, Ernest, Julius and Mr Cohen met in the home of Mr Cohen's Christian friends. For four hours Ernest and Julius answered his questions and explained to him the way of salvation. By 6pm, Katz – who described himself as "a spiritual midwife" – felt they had talked long enough and that it was time for Mr Cohen to make a decision. Katz suggested that they get on their knees and, after he and Ernest had prayed, he asked if Mr Cohen was ready to ask Jesus to forgive his sins. Mr Cohen was deeply moved. He had been convinced of the truth of their faith. They had something which, he admitted, was worth having. He envied the joy that they and his daughter possessed, and he wanted it too. However, to submit to the lordship of Jesus would cost him dearly. He could not act impulsively. He had to consider his family, his people, his social position and his financial affairs; everything hung on his decision.

Katz assured Mr Cohen that he could have the same peace, joy and assurance he and Ernest had. "Not now, my brethren," said Mr Cohen, "there is so much to consider." He then added that before he met Ernest and Julius he had wished with all his heart that Rebekah would renounce her newly found faith in Christ, and he had hoped they would support him; now he wanted her to continue in her faith. He asked the two missionaries to pray that strength and courage would be granted to him to receive Jesus as his Saviour soon.

The following Saturday Mr Cohen and Julius Katz met in the same parlour. Ernest had a speaking engagement and was unable to join them. Mr Cohen wanted to know how Julius became a believer in Jesus and why he had left the synagogue. Katz told him of his orthodox upbringing, his search for the Truth, and how Jesus found him and gave him eternal life. He then asked if Mr Cohen had resolved his inner conflict. He had not. He knew he had to believe in Jesus, but he could not do so at that time.

Katz listened patiently for two hours, advising and encouraging the troubled Jew. Finally he said, "Mr Cohen, I am sure you should make your salvation certain today. Tomorrow may be too late. I agree it costs much, but think what it cost Christ to redeem us. I cannot convert you, neither can I compel you to be converted. It is your loss if you reject Him; and your attitude is a rejection. The Word of God warns us, 'How shall we escape if we neglect so great salvation?' I cannot see that it serves any purpose to continue our conversation today. Let us pray together and then we will separate."

Katz knelt and prayed that God would open Mr Cohen's eyes and grant him to trust Jesus as his Saviour. He prayed also for his wife and family and especially for Rebekah. Still on his knees, Katz invited Mr Cohen to pray also. The orthodox Jew rose from the sofa and prayed: "Heavenly Father, I thank Thee for bringing me in touch with my Hebrew brethren who believe in Jesus Christ and say He is the Messiah. I know they are honest people, they know what they are talking about. They have a joy I cannot understand, and in my soul it is dark. I have no peace; I am utterly miserable and I have no atonement for my sins. Everything they say I feel is true, but I cannot understand it. And yet my own Rebekah understands and believes it. Thou canst reveal it unto me. Thou knowest I want to be honest with Thee, with my brethren and myself. I have not yet the light, but I know it will come one day. I thank Thee for all Thy blessings upon me and my family. Amen."

Katz pleaded with him to ask the Lord Jesus to forgive his sins and make him a child of God.

"No, not now, I don't want to be dishonest. I can't do it now."

He walked with Katz to the bus stop, where they separated. Julius was deeply saddened but, at about 11.30 that same night, as Mr Cohen was sitting with his Christian friends, he suddenly cried out, "He is mine! Jesus Christ is my Redeemer! I know He is mine! I must go home at once and tell my family that Jesus is mine!"

When Mr Cohen broke the news of his faith in Jesus, Rebekah wept for joy. Mr Cohen's eldest son was overcome with rage and slapped his father across the face, calling him a *meshummad*. The son packed his bags immediately, called a taxi and left home. Mrs Cohen embraced her husband, assuring him through her tears that he was her husband and she would never leave him. She did not understand what had happened to her daughter and husband but she was willing to learn and promised to start reading the New Testament.

The following morning, as Julius Katz was on his way to speak at the Iron Hall in Belfast, Ernest told him the good news. The next time they met, Julius greeted Mr Cohen with the words of Job: "I know that my Redeemer liveth."

"So do I", said Ernest.

"And so do I!" said Mr Cohen, "I know that my Redeemer liveth!"

The Importance of Being Ernest

They embraced each other and, before they parted, they committed the Cohen family to the Lord. Little wonder then, that after such a remarkable, sovereign work of the Holy Spirit, Ernest could face whatever the future had in store for him.

7

Brylcreem and toothpaste

Send thou men, that they may
search the land... (Numbers 13:2)

The Dutch settlers who took part in the Great Trek in the
nineteenth century saw themselves as Israelites and South
Africa as their Promised Land. Their British enemies were
their Egyptian persecutors and the black inhabitants of the
land were godless Canaanites to be exterminated or
subjugated. That skewed worldview paved the way for the
godless system of apartheid, in which black South Africans
were second-class citizens, fit only to be "hewers of wood
and drawers of water" for their white masters. On Thursday
1st March 1951, Ernest stepped ashore in Cape Town from
the SS Cape Town Castle as an Israelite indeed, a Joshua
with a mission to spy out the land on behalf of one greater
than Moses. He would return to Britain on 31st August, but
his six months in South Africa would result in the
establishment of one of the most fruitful branches of the
British Jews Society.

Two weeks previously, he had left a monochrome England

in the grip of an icy winter. Here, at ten in the morning, a dazzling sun hung in an azure sky above Table Mountain and the heat almost overpowered him. For fourteen days he had shared a windowless three-berth cabin at the ship's stern, above the engine room. Nevertheless, the voyage had been pleasant and invigorating and had provided opportunities to share the gospel with his fellow passengers. There were twenty other Christians aboard. Each evening they met for Bible study, and on both Sundays at sea they held a Sunday School and a gospel service.

Two weeks after Ernest arrived, his old friend Frank Exley, who was at that time the Society's Superintendent of the London Missions, died at the age of 84. Exley's passing marked the end of an era for the society just as a new era of expansion was commencing with Ernest's South African visit.

As he emerged from Customs, a stranger approached him and asked if he was Mr Lloyd of the British Jews Society. Ernest said he was and immediately found his hand in the firm grip of A.J.W. Rowland, a man known and loved throughout South Africa. "A warm welcome to South Africa, and may the Lord richly bless your visit!" Rowland made it his practice to welcome every Christian minister who arrived in Cape Town, and soon Ernest was being driven down the beautiful King George VI Walk into the city itself and on to the home of his host and hostess, Dr and Mrs Salzberg.

For the whole of March, Ernest spoke at churches in and around Cape Town. His first meeting was at Bethany Hall, from where Leslie Gay, a Geordie, was reaching out with the compassion of Christ to the black community. While in South Africa, Ernest kept a journal of his travels, and in the June issue of the *Missionary Herald*, his diary was published under the heading, *Deputation Notes*.

Sunday March 4th, was my first Sunday in South Africa, and the morning found me at Pinelands Baptist Church, where I enjoyed happy fellowship and found a most attentive congregation. Pinelands is a lovely suburb similar to Welwyn Garden City. I had two Jewish Christians in the congregation, Mrs. Smoljar and Mr. John During. In the afternoon I spoke at Seapoint, a coastal resort, where there are many Jews, and after the meeting I had a talk with a fine young Jewish student who had listened with interest. At night, accompanied by dear Mr. Rowland, I visited the Lady Michaelus Hospital and gave a talk to the nursing staff.

Monday March 5th. In the afternoon I was given a great reception at the weekly prayer meeting organised by Mr. Rowland at Wale Street Baptist Church, and was given my passport to Cape Town – a stick of rock! I was able to give a talk about our work to a most interested audience. I had that same evening, in the home of Mr. John During, a meeting of representatives of all the Jewish Missions of the Cape. It was a welcome to me personally and to our Society. The greeting of the Dutch Reformed Church Mission to Israel was voiced by Rev. Mr. Lutski, a real lover of Israel. Mr. Eddie Levine, representing the Hadderech Jewish Christian Youth Movement, then spoke. Mr. John During followed. A warm welcome was also given by the Prayer Union for Israel, and then Dr. Salzberg, who presided, gave the greetings of the Hebrew Christian Alliance of South Africa. I then gave an address on our work and the need of bringing Christ to Israel. This was an excellent meeting at which we were indeed "All one in Christ Jesus".

March 6th. At 10.30 am. I spoke to the Baptist Women's Association at Claremont Baptist Church, where the good lady of the Manse, Mrs. Herringshaw, presided over the meeting. A splendid meeting. At night I was in lovely country out at Paarl, the centre of the Vines district. The meeting was held amongst our good friends of the Dutch Reformed Church with the Assistant Minister, Rev. Dr. J. L. De Villiers, presiding.

March 7th. I was taken to a Fruit Farm near Paarl. It was a very hot day and I saw and also picked many delicious fruits, including figs, peaches and apricots. In the afternoon, at a small village school I spoke to a group of farmers and their wives. At night I was back at Claremont Baptist Church where the good Minister, Rev. H. Herringshaw, gave our Mission such a warm welcome.

March 8th. 10.30 a.m. I gave a talk at the African Evangelistic Band training college in Glenvar. What a good crowd of students, and how appreciatively they listened. The Lord bless them and dear Miss Mary Bazeley, whose mother in Cornwall is such a friend of our work. A splendid meeting at night at the YWCA, under the auspices of the Berean Band. A hall full of people who were most interested as I told of our work. The Chairman, Mr. Noel Rowland, M.A., is a great lover of Israel. We had more than one unsaved Jew in that night, and they listened attentively.

March 10th. I was again at Bethany Hall, where I gave a Bible Reading which was appreciated by the coloured audience.

March 11th. My day began with a talk to the girls at the YWCA, and I had a good time, not only pleading the cause of Israel, but also the claims of the Lord Jesus Christ as Saviour. At 10.30 am I had a wonderful congregation in the Wale Street Baptist Church, Cape Town. The service was full of the presence of Christ, and it was a joy to minister to such a congregation. What a joy to meet so many friends of Israel afterwards. At 4.30 and 7.30pm I had packed meetings at Bethany Hall.

March 12th. A good drawing room meeting in the home of Mr. and Mrs. Schroeder, with unconverted people in. I feel that work for the Kingdom was done that night.

March 13th. I had the great joy of giving the first of two talks at the Bible Institute at Kalk Bay – a most lovely suburb. The Principal, Rev. S. Law, M.A., from Bonnie Scotland, has a fine college and a grand crowd of students. There was a question time afterwards. God bless this excellent college and prosper all concerned. At night I spoke to the Nursing staff at the Booth Memorial Hospital, with the Matron, Miss Foxton, in the chair.

March 14th. I spoke at a factory lunchtime meeting and witnessed to the power of Christ to save and redeem both Jew and Gentile. At night I was at the Methodist Church, Simonstown.

March 15th. 11.45am. A meeting with the Pinelands Baptist Women's Association. What a joy to meet at lunch that day, Mr. Martin from London. A new friendship made which, I trust, will live for a long while. At night I spoke at the Carinus Home for Nurses.

March 16th. In the morning I gave a word at a prayer meeting in the home of Mrs. Fairweather, a dear lover of Israel. At night an excellent drawing room meeting in the home of Mrs. Ball and her daughter. The interest was very real here.

March 17th. A splendid meeting at Vish Hock with our friends of the Open Brethren.

March 18th. In the morning I again occupied the pulpit of Wale Street Baptist Church. The Church was quite full. I shall never forget the grand spirit that prevailed there. At night I had a meal with the Rev. and Mrs. Killick at Muizenberg, at the Methodist Manse. Two grand Christians who made me most welcome. At night I took the service in their Church, and again many were for the first time interested in the Jewish people and their salvation through Christ.

March 19th. I went to give the second talk at the Kalk Bay Bible College, and again felt thrilled to be in such an atmosphere. I shall not easily forget these two occasions. At night I spoke at the Pinelands Gospel Hall, when friends became interested in our work.

March 20th. Mrs. Killick took the chair at a meeting in the home of one of the Methodist ladies. At night we had a splendid meeting in the Methodist Church.

March 21st. I had a fine meeting at Wynberg Baptist Church where the good minister, Rev. F. Mason, gave our Mission such a warm welcome. Many friends were present who have a real love for the Covenant People.

The next few days were spent by the sea in beautiful Somerset West, amidst pine trees and mountains at the United Evangelical Camp. A hundred and twenty people, mostly youth, were present for five talks – three Bible readings on a Jewish theme, a "Camp Fire talk" and a Sunday evening gospel address. Before Ernest was allowed to speak to the campers, he had to undergo an initiation ordeal that took the form of a trial by jury. He was indicted for abandoning his wife and children, and the verdict (inevitably) was "Guilty" and sentence was passed. He was to be anointed with a noxious blend of hair oil and toothpaste. The mixture was applied vigorously by a group of zealous youngsters and, in the heat of the South African summer night, it stung his scalp and face. But every ear was open as he addressed them for the first time, and in the next few days a half dozen people – amongst them a Jewish woman – made professions of faith, and many more indicated a desire to renew their Christian commitment.

On the final evening, Good Friday, Ernest spoke about "full surrender to the Lord and implicit obedience to His Divine will". Among the 120 campers were Eddie and Eunice Levine of the Hadderech Jewish Christian Youth Movement. Eddie was an Egyptian Jew and his wife Eunice South African. Eddie's family disowned him after he became a Christian and threw him physically out of the house. Eddie and Eunice wanted to work as missionaries amongst their own people, but until that time they had not known which mission agency they should approach. They felt that Ernest was speaking directly to them and, at the end of the evening, they approached him to discuss the possibility of their working with the British Jews Society. Ernest arranged for papers to be sent from the UK, and at the next meeting of the BJS Council the application of Eddie and Eunice Levine came up for consideration with Ernest's full recommendation. By the time he left South Africa, the British Jews Society had its first missionaries in the country.

However, the BJS had more than just their first missionaries. Three days before Ernest left Cape Town, Eddie had his first two evangelistic contacts when two very irate students from the university confronted him and Ernest. They had heard Ernest state at an open-air meeting that Jesus was in the 22nd Psalm. "You're mad!" one of them shouted, shaking his fist in Ernest's face. "Psalm 22 is just pastoral poetry!"

Ernest managed to calm him down enough to ask a question. "On the Day of Atonement you pray from Psalm 51, 'Create in me a clean heart, O God'. Are those words just 'pastoral poetry'?"

"No, they're not!"

Ernest challenged him over the lack of consistency in his argument, but the young man came back with a bitter attack on the Christian view of salvation. He maintained that, "salvation lies within". Ernest asked the student to prove his assertion from the Hebrew Scriptures, pointing out that in Leviticus 17:11 God told Moses that blood makes atonement for the soul.

"I'm not a butcher." said the young man. "I've no time for all that nonsense!"

Ernest was puzzled. If the young Jew was not religious, why was he defending traditional Judaism so vehemently? The student's anger cooled and he confessed that he was very religious.

After Ernest left Cape Town, Eddie Levine maintained contact with the student, and some weeks later Ernest received a letter from Eddie saying the young man had begun to read the New Testament.

It was not only students that Ernest disturbed. A feisty

Jewish lady informed him after a church service that it was a pity someone hadn't killed him at birth. "Fancy a Jewish man believing in all that Jesus stuff!" she said.

Ernest asked if she was *frum* – strict in her religious observance. She replied that she was.

Did she recite the *Shema* every morning – *Shema Yisrael, Adonai Eloheinu, echad Adonai* – "Hear, O Israel, the LORD our God, the LORD is one" (Deuteronomy 6:4)? She confessed that she didn't.

Did she attend *shul* – synagogue – regularly? Only on high days and holy days.

"Well," he said, "you're not exactly *religious*, are you? You seem to go to *shul* just to remind yourself that you're Yiddish."

She warmed to the straight-talking missionary and Ernest's hosts invited her to visit him in their home. Ernest advised them not to offer her food because she would eat only *kosher* food, and he requested them to stay out of the conversation unless he asked them a question.

The lady arrived and the conversation quickly became very animated and heated. Nevertheless, when Ernest had to move on, she was sad to see him leave and asked him to write to her. In her letters, she bombarded him with questions. She put forth the standard objections to Christianity, but she also wanted to know why the Levitical sacrifices had ceased and why, in spite of the fact that beautiful prayers are recited on Yom Kippur, the Day of Atonement, Jewish people have no peace.

Ernest answered her questions and sent her a Bible, counselling her not to bother with the New Testament until she had read the Old Testament, and telling her to write to him if she had any questions. Many Christians would question his wisdom. Are the Jewish people not already familiar with the Old Testament? Would it not have been better to get her straight to the Gospels? In answer, it was evident from their discussions that the woman had no knowledge of the Old Testament, the writings God gave as a preparation for the coming of the Messiah. Therefore, to circumvent Moses and the Prophets by going straight to the New Testament would have been the spiritual equivalent of building a house from the roof down. Some years later, when Ernest was in Cape Town again, a friend told him of a Jewish lady who had joined his church and wanted to know if he knew a Mr Lloyd from London, because something he preached had made her come to the Messiah. It was the same lady.

In Durban, one of South Africa's leading Zionists attended a meeting at which Ernest was speaking, and they later met to talk. The man was eminently reasonable, but admitted that he had always imagined a Jew who changed his creed was either mentally deficient or was motivated by a desire for material advantage. Ernest was no intellectual lightweight; he was well read, articulate in conversation and totally sincere in his commitment to his beliefs. The Zionist conceded that there might, after all, be something in what Ernest believed.

In Johannesburg, entire suburbs were almost exclusively Jewish, and it was a centre for both Orthodox Judaism and Zionism. Not for nothing was it nicknamed "Jewburg". Ernest was deeply concerned that little was being done to reach the Jewish people of Johannesburg with the gospel. He was heartened, however, by the constant pleas from the churches to commence a work in the city. A fellow Jewish believer appealed with tears in his eyes for the BJS to "do something for the Jewish people in Johannesburg".

On 3rd April 1952, less than six months after Ernest's return to the UK, a valedictory service was held at the

Livingstone Hall in London for Julius Katz and his wife. Until this time, the stocky, moon-faced Katz had been the BJS missionary in Liverpool, and when the request came for him to head up the work in South Africa, his response was that he would go where the Lord wanted him to go. Katz combined a deep spirituality with a brusque but engaging personality. He described himself in his thick accent as "a spiritual midwife bringink many sons to glory; sometimes der births are very painful but a joy it is to see spiritual children growink into der Messiah."

The partnership of Julius Katz and Eddie Levine in South Africa was on a par with the teaming of Stan Laurel and Oliver Hardy, both physically and in terms of personality. Together, Katz and Levine travelled thousands of miles every year in a Gospel Van, Eddie driving while Katz, the senior man, navigated and gave orders. On their way to one of their many meetings, Eddie Levine was not convinced that Katz's navigation was sound. Katz made it clear that he was the director and knew what he was doing. He ordered Eddie to pull up outside an imposing church building.

"But Meester Katz" Eddie protested in his high voice, "dees ees der wrong church!"

"Ach, Eddie, be quiet; I'm der director."

Moments later Katz realised they were in a Roman Catholic church.

"Eddie, vhy are ve in der wrong church? Vhy didn't you tell me?"

"Meester Katz, I told you eet was wrong…"

"Eddie, you are talkink to der person who runs der verk!"

On another occasion, Katz instructed Eddie, who would be sitting in the audience, to tap his watch to remind him if he spoke over a certain amount of time. At the appointed time Eddie dutifully lifted his left hand and tapped his watch.

Katz appeared not to have seen him and continued speaking. Eddie tapped his watch with more exaggerated movements. Katz took no notice. Eddie's right hand began to move in wide arcs as he tried to attract the attention of his director. Katz stopped in mid sentence: "Eddie, vhy are you distractink me? Please sit down and be quiet!"

*****

The BJS work in South Africa grew so rapidly that in 1953 it became the South Africa Society for the Propagation of the Gospel among the Jews. By the following year the South African branch was entirely self-supporting and began to provide financial support for the work of the BJS in Haifa, Israel. In 1959, the BJS appointed Rev. C.J. Mundell as the South Africa Field Director, and under his direction the work grew and prospered. Jack Mundell, himself a Hebrew Christian, travelled widely throughout the country promoting the work, and reports of Jewish people finding the Messiah were received regularly.

One of the most notable Jewish personalities to come to faith in South Africa was the singer Al Preston. When Eddie Levine visited him in hospital, Preston asked bitterly why God had ruined his promising career by afflicting him with crippling arthritis. Eddie simply asked him to put his complete trust in God, confess that he was a sinner and ask the Lord Jesus Christ to come into his life. Hardly realising what he was saying, Al Preston repeated a prayer after Eddie. Preston went on to become an evangelist, broadcasting evangelistic messages for Jewish people on South African radio and recording a number of gospel albums.

Within ten years of Ernest's exploratory tour, the South Africa branch of the BJS was the largest, apart from that in the UK. By 1962, the mission consisted of a President and two committees, one in Cape Town and the other in Durban, a Field Director, three missionaries (including Eddie Levine) in Johannesburg, two in Cape Town, and one each in Durban and Bloemfontein. The South African branch also supplied a worker for the medical work in Haifa in the person of Dr Brian Pockroy.

The success of the South African mission ensured that pioneer missionary work would be the future shape of Ernest's ministry and that, until his retirement, he would hardly ever be at home.

8
Down Under

*Ye shall be witnesses unto me ... unto the
uttermost part of the earth.* (Acts 1:8)

Encouraged by the success of the South Africa venture, Will
Newton phoned Ernest in 1952: "Would it be all right for me
to tell the Council you are willing to go to Australia and New
Zealand next year?"

"Let me talk to Jessie."

Jessie's response was immediate and definite: "Well you
go, don't you!"

In the nineteen fifties, there was no organised Christian
witness to the thinly spread Jewish community in New
Zealand, and Ernest had no contacts in Australia except the
New South Wales Mission to the Jews based in Sydney. His
brief was to explore the possibilities of establishing a branch
of the BJS in both those countries. It would mean being away
from March to October, and the most economical way to the
antipodes was on the P&O Line from Tilbury in London to
Fremantle in Western Australia, a voyage of about one month.
At the valedictory service, Will Newton commended Ernest
to the prayers of BJS supporters:

God laid His hand upon him long, long ago to make him a chosen vessel for a particular service with the B.J.S., as a representative of the Society, bearing the Society's name and reputation in his hands as he goes from place to place. He has been doing this admirably well for something like twenty years. Now we have come to a point where he is chosen, and I believe chosen of the Lord, for a special mission, for a great task. He is being presented with a great opportunity but also with a tremendous responsibility, for, as you all know, the B.J.S. is forward looking and outward looking, as well as upward looking. We believe the present age is not so very different, if different at all, from any other age in which the Church has found itself. In every age there have been difficulties, problems, headaches and heartaches, and we are getting our particular kind. But we are also being given the grace to face our difficulties, and Mr. Lloyd has quite readily and willingly, in strong faith, assumed this burden. He is going to Australia to pioneer and I should like to ask for your prayers for the task that lies before him. So far as the B.J.S. is concerned it is virgin soil. We are not known to many friends in Australia.

As Mr. Lloyd goes to Perth, Adelaide, Melbourne, Tasmania, Brisbane, Sydney, Wellington, Auckland, Dunedin and Christchurch, he is going to totally new fields to investigate the general position and also make known the work and stir the people of God to a sense of their responsibility to the Jewish people. He is pioneering just as he did in South Africa. It will be a lengthy task. It will take six months and that is a long time to be away, and so far away.

On 12th March 1953, he set sail from Tilbury on the S.S.

Stratheard. Jessie, Peter, Martin and Jennifer said goodbye to him at St. Pancras Station; they would not see him again until November. As with his trip to South Africa, Ernest travelled in the cheapest quarters, a small rear cabin shared with four other men, two of whom returned to the cabin each night totally inebriated. There were several stops on the way, and when the ship docked for three days in Bombay, he was met by John Buffam, a Canadian, who invited him to assist him in his work among the Jewish community for the duration of the stopover. A taxi was waiting for them and the driver wanted to know immediately if Ernest had the money for the fare. He replied that his friend was paying. The driver wanted to know what Ernest was doing in India and he answered that he was on his way to Australia and New Zealand to preach. What would he preach about? The Jews, he replied. How could he preach about the Jews? Ernest responded that the Old Testament was a wonderful story full of Jewish history.

The driver was Jewish but had an interest in all religions; he believed the solution to the world's problems was to be found in all faiths. Did Ernest not believe that? Ernest asked what the driver would think if he was ill and the doctor prescribed fifty different medicines to be taken together? He explained that Jewish people, like everyone else, were suffering from a spiritual malady for which there was only one remedy.

John Buffam's evident love for the Jewish people and the simplicity of his lifestyle impressed Ernest. The Jews of Bombay were known as the *Benei Israelis*, "the sons of Israel". Two things stood out about these religiously observant Jews: they were very Indian in appearance and extremely poor. John Buffam lived in a very humble home among the *Benei Israelis*, and on the Friday evening he took Ernest to visit some friends. They arrived just as the mother was kindling the candles to welcome the Sabbath into the home.

The Sabbath is an important element of Jewish life. It commences at sunset on Friday, when all work must cease and the family comes together for the Sabbath meal. Some of the Jewish sages taught that the command to keep the Sabbath was the most important of all, equal to the keeping of all the other commandments. So meritorious is Sabbath observance that some of the great rabbis taught that if all Israel kept one Sabbath perfectly, the Messiah would come. According to Orthodox Jewish authorities, the time of lighting the Sabbath candles is especially propitious for praying for health and happiness, because the prayer is offered during the performance of this great *mitzvah*, or meritorious deed.

The father invited Ernest and John to join the family for the Sabbath meal. He broke the traditional plaited *challa* bread, sprinkled salt on it and handed it to Ernest, a gesture which both surprised and moved him. In the East, the "salt of the covenant" is still the supreme gesture of hospitality. The Psalmist lamented that his familiar friend who ate of his salt lifted up his heel against him. To do someone harm after eating the salt of the covenant with them was the consummate act of betrayal. However earnestly his Indian Jewish host might disagree with him during their arguments that evening, Ernest knew he was among friends. He had nothing to fear from this family.

At another home, a beautiful Indian Jewish woman appeared at the door with her two sons. Buffam introduced Ernest as a Jew who believed in the Messiah.

"He thinks he will convert us?" she smiled.

Ernest replied that he had never converted anyone and hoped he never would. Only God could truly convert. She invited them in for coffee – Turkish coffee – thick enough to stand a spoon in and strong enough to keep a man awake for a week. But it was another gesture of hospitality. The *Benei Israelis* may have been poor, but they were generous and hospitable.

During a brief stopover in Ceylon, now Sri Lanka, the Brethren Hall in Colombo invited Ernest to speak about the work of the British Jews Society. B.P. Fernandes, the President of the Bible Society of Ceylon introduced Ernest to a number of other churches in Colombo, a gesture that prepared the way for future visits to the country. In a night temperature of 100°F, with his clothes soaked with perspiration, he spoke about the work of the British Jews Society at a meeting where a young Jewish woman was present. Afterwards, she approached him to say that when he began to speak she was angry. She felt he had betrayed the Jewish people but, by the time he finished his address, she sensed that he truly loved his people. She was troubled because her marriage to a Brahmin was disintegrating. She would not give up her Judaism while he refused to let go of his Hinduism. Ernest assured her that he was not asking her to "give up" Judaism; he was pointing her to the one in whom Judaism finds its fulfilment and who can satisfy the longings of Jewish hearts. They spoke only briefly, but before he returned to the UK, he learned that each Sunday since his visit she had attended the Gospel Service at a Brethren Hall and that her attitude to Jesus had softened noticeably. If at any time she were unable to attend, she would send a letter of explanation.

*****

Ernest disembarked in Fremantle to discover that news of his coming had preceded him. He was greeted by the Rev. Jim Hendry, the Secretary of the Western Australian Baptist Union, who asked where he was staying. Hendry, who was born and raised in Glasgow and trained at the Bible Training Institute – now the International Christian College – was indignant when Ernest said he planned to find a room at the YMCA. He insisted that Ernest stay at his home, and provided him with an office in the Baptist Union headquarters, from where he was able to make contact with churches throughout Western Australia. Within three days of setting foot on Australian soil, he had arranged speaking engagements for every night of his first month, and by the time he completed his tour of Australasia he had addressed over three hundred meetings. The only break from his punishing schedule came when he managed to fit in a single game of badminton after an evening meeting.

Shortly after Ernest arrived in the country, a Jewish lady called on the Hendrys. Jim's wife introduced her to Ernest and, upon discovering the purpose of his visit to Australia, she suggested cynically that he must be making a lot of money or else he would not be doing the work. Ernest asked if she really believed he would leave his wife and children for months on end for the sake of a good salary. She apologised. She explained that she was German and that the Nazis had murdered her parents and husband. Were it not for the kindness and courage of Christians, she and her two children would never have escaped from Germany. In Australia, the Jewish authorities helped her, and she was afraid in case they should think she had any sympathy with Christianity. She admitted she was reading the New Testament and, during the following weeks, she attended two of Ernest's meetings.

He was accompanied on his travels on the west coast by Hebrew Christian, Alfred Abrams. As far as Abrams knew, there were no other Jewish believers in Western Australia, and he was delighted to make contact with Ernest. At the meetings, Ernest preached and spoke about the work of the

BJS while Abrams told the story of how he found the Messiah. Most Christians in Western Australia had never encountered Jews who believed in Jesus and had probably never heard of Hebrew Christians, so two Jewish believers together made a considerable impact.

In Fremantle, Ernest received a letter from the Jewish Evangelical Witness, a mission to Jewish people based in Adelaide in South Australia. Far from seeing him as a competitor, they had arranged two weeks of meetings for Ernest in a variety of churches and, after a month in Fremantle, he set out for Adelaide.

Australia is a vast country, and for some reason that no one has yet been able to fathom, every state has its own rail gauge. Ernest took the overnight train from Perth to the old gold-mining town of Kalgoorlie on a three-foot-six gauge which, he recalls, "was like riding a concertina". He arrived in Kalgoorlie on Friday and at 10.30am boarded the train to Adelaide. During the fifteen hundred mile journey across the Nullarbor Plain – on what is still the longest straight stretch of railway in the world – there was no air conditioning and the heat was stifling. Four days later Ernest stepped off the train exhausted. He was greeted by a tiny Yorkshire lady who knew the BJS workers in Leeds, and who had lost none of her accent: "Aye, lad. Welcome t' thee."

His meetings in Adelaide were mainly at Brethren halls and Baptist churches, but in addition to his speaking activities in churches, he was actively involved in evangelism with workers of the Jewish Evangelical Witness. In the BJS magazine, he reported an incident that occurred while he was speaking at the Anglican Holy Trinity Church one Wednesday night. As the meeting began, two Jewish ladies walked in. They both sat in the front and the elder of the two said, loud enough to be heard, "He's mad!"

The younger whispered, with obvious embarrassment, "Mother, be quiet! You are not in synagogue; you are in church now!"

"There's only one God!" the mother shouted.

Though Judaism has never formulated an extensive authoritative theology, the basic confession of faith among Jewish people has traditionally been the words of Deuteronomy 6:4: "Hear, O Israel: The LORD our God is one LORD." It is a common misconception among Jewish people that Christians believe in three gods and, therefore, to become a follower of Jesus is to become a worshipper of other gods. Ernest was unruffled and interrupted his talk to address her: "Madam, I'm prepared to talk to you after the meeting but you wouldn't like it if one of these people came to *shul* next Saturday and shouted at the rabbi."

After the meeting, Mrs Goldstein approached him. "I like you." she said.

Ernest laughed: "You didn't at first!"

She asked if he would go to her home for a meal. Ernest said he would be delighted to accept her invitation. Mrs Goldstein was a widow, but her husband had left her well provided for. She was religiously orthodox and observed the strict kosher dietary regulations laid down by the rabbis, which included not eating meat from unclean animals and the separation of meat and dairy products. The house was furnished sumptuously with antiques, which she showed off with great enthusiasm and in which Ernest showed genuine interest. The Goldstein children were very accomplished: one of the sons was a doctor, the other a dentist and the daughter was a solicitor. Mrs Goldstein wanted to know where Ernest was staying and when he told her he was with a Christian minister, she was shocked. How could a Jew be *frum* in a gentile house? The food would be contaminated.

He responded that there was more to being religious than having a *kosher* kitchen and asked if she minded him quoting Jesus.

"If you like." she replied.

He reminded her that Jesus was Jewish and, as such, ate *kosher* all the time, but he taught it was not what went into men that defiled them, but what came out of their hearts. Why did Jewish people think everything hung on the ceremonial? The inside mattered, not the outside. *Frum* Jews were concerned about kosher food and the external rituals of Judaism, but Ernest wished that they were as concerned for their souls as they were for their *kosher* orthodoxy.

Her son, the doctor, said he had heard that Jews who turned to Christianity received a gift of $50,000.

Mrs Goldstein turned on him sharply: "You're very rude! Mr Lloyd is my guest and you will treat him with respect!"

After the meal, she asked what Ernest got "out of all this". She was not thinking in financial terms. Mrs Goldstein wanted to know if believing in Jesus really helped him. Earlier in the evening she had shared with him that when her husband died, she felt as though her whole world had collapsed and she had no hope. He assured Mrs Goldstein that if his world crumbled around him and he was left with nothing, he knew that Messiah would be with him and would never forsake him.

"Even if life goes dead against you?"

Even if life went "dead against" him, Ernest knew that Messiah would be always with him.

They met several times during his stay in Adelaide, and Mrs Goldstein and her daughter attended another of his meetings. By the time he left Adelaide, mother and daughter were both "definite enquirers" and the door was open for workers of the Jewish Evangelical Witness to visit them.

There were other encouragements in Adelaide. He recorded a number of broadcasts for the local radio station 5KA, and at the Grange Christian Centre a young woman was converted. From Adelaide he travelled to Melbourne, again by rail as it was the cheapest form of travel. There were no sleeping facilities and he arrived exhausted in Melbourne, where he was pleasantly surprised to be hailed by the secretary of the Sudan Interior Mission, Mr Quintin, and his wife. Quintin had heard of Ernest's arrival ahead of time, and laid on accommodation at the SIM mission home and arranged meetings for him. The Quintins were well-intentioned, but when it became apparent to Ernest that the interest of the churches was not so much in Jewish mission as in the newly-founded state of Israel and the prophetic future of the Jewish people, his excitement waned. In a rare fit of negativity, Ernest recorded in the BJS *Herald* that he had passed from a warm atmosphere of kindness in Adelaide "to quite another climate in Melbourne and Victoria where I cannot say I waxed enthusiastic over time spent there."

It was his policy never to decline an invitation to speak, wherever it might be, or at whatever time of the day or night it might be scheduled. However, there were times in Melbourne when he came close to regretting his policy. Many churches wanted exciting stories or prophetic addresses. The minister of one church informed him before he spoke that they were expecting a "story of revival" from him.

In 1953, the state of Israel was five years old. She had emerged triumphant from a war of aggression launched by her Arab neighbours on the day she declared her independence, and had made her presence felt on the stage of international affairs. Christians were excited because they saw the re-establishment of the tiny nation state as a fulfilment of the prophecies of the ancient Hebrew prophets. Many

Christians had looked forward, as much as the Jews themselves, to the day when the Jewish people would return to their ancient homeland, and among the churches of Melbourne interest in Israel was high. People wanted to know if Ernest was a missionary in Israel and what his opinions were on the prophetic significance of the re-establishment of the people in their own land. His own concerns, however, were different. No doubt reflecting on his experiences in Melbourne, Ernest wrote in the June 1954 BJS *Herald*:

> I am often asked on my wanderings the most obtuse questions regarding the future of Israel. I prefer to deal with the present. Israel needs Christ and we, in the Society and other Jewish missions, feel our responsibility is not to live in future days but today to be an evangelistic witness to the Jewish people. I wish that the Christian Church were as concerned for the present conditions of Israel as they are for their future conditions. It is Israel's soul that matters.

There were some 60,000 Jews in Melbourne, and Mount Scopus, named after the hill to the south east of Jerusalem, was the largest school in the city. Ernest was dismayed to discover that the churches were making no attempts to reach these people with the gospel. The Jewish Evangelical Witness had a representative in the city whose radio talks on Judaism were very popular. Dr Lawrence Duff-Forbes was fluent in both biblical and modern Hebrew and wore full Jewish garb for his broadcasts, including a *kippah*, the round skullcap worn by orthodox men, and a *tallit*, or prayer shawl. When Ernest visited him, Duff-Forbes welcomed him very graciously but made it clear that his objectives differed from those of his guest. It was apparent that his interests lay more in the observance of Shabbat and the festivals than in evangelism, and he saw Ernest's presence in the city as an intrusion into his territory. Duff-Forbes was an early advocate of what would become known as Messianic Judaism. He later moved to California, where he commenced a ministry called *Israel's Anchorage* and *Yeshivat Yahadut Meshichi* – the Academy of Messianic Judaism – a training programme attended by one who would in later years become a luminary in the Messianic movement, Edward Brotsky.

Nevertheless, there were encouragements in Melbourne. Although Ernest was not a member of the Brethren assemblies, they there welcomed him. Notwithstanding their interest in Israel and prophecy, they were keen to know what was being done to point Jewish people to their Messiah.

From Melbourne he sailed to Tasmania, nineteen hours and 280 miles by ship across the Bass Strait, where he was met by a very young, newly married couple, David and Pat McCormack. The McCormacks and Ernest had never met before and Ernest had no idea what they looked like, except that he had imagined them to be elderly. The three became friends instantly and have remained so for half a century. David and Pat named two of their sons after him, Timothy Lloyd McCormack and Christopher Lloyd McCormack. Of all the places he visited in Australia, Ernest loved Tasmania the most, not only because of its magnificent mountainous scenery and weather, which reminded him of Scotland, but above all because of David and Pat, who were wedded to Jewish mission and made him part of their family.

David was a member of a Brethren assembly and had sufficient influence to introduce Ernest to a number of other assemblies, where he was enthusiastically received. He met no Jewish people in Tasmania, but invitations for him to speak to groups of Christians came thick and fast, including requests from a number of schools who were intrigued to discover that there were missionaries to the Jewish people.

*****

In Brisbane, 1,600 miles to the north by sea and rail, he was invited to speak at the Christian Union meeting. Fifteen or sixteen unconverted Jewish students were present, all of whom were under the impression that missions gained Jewish converts by means of material inducement. Ernest took as his subject the conversion of Saul of Tarsus, using as his background the recently published novel *The Apostle,* by the acclaimed Yiddish writer, Sholem Asch. Though Asch was, and is, greatly respected by the Jewish literary establishment, his great "Christological" trilogy – *The Nazarene, The Apostle* and *Mary,* published in 1939, 1943 and 1949 respectively – was heavily criticised by the Jewish establishment. The Yiddish daily, *Forward,* to which Asch had been a regular contributor, not only refused to publish the work, but also attacked the author for "encouraging heresy and conversion by preaching Christianity". In the early 1950s, Asch's trilogy was still a talking point in the Jewish community, and after the talk a young Jewish couple shared with Ernest that though they could not agree with all he had said, they were of the opinion that the demands of the Jewish people could be met only by the religion of the New Testament.

Some of Ernest's greatest encouragements were found in the churches and fellowships of Brisbane. At a ladies' meeting held in one of the Brethren halls, he was treated to a huge and sumptuous breakfast of crayfish, after which he spoke about the work of the British Jews Society and then invited questions. One of the seventy women present rose to make a statement. "Many of us," she said feelingly, "did not know this work among the Jews was going on. It is no good our saying to Mr. Lloyd, 'Thank you very much for an interesting morning.' It is time we did something about this. What are we going to do about helping Jewish evangelisation?" Similar responses came from other meetings, and before he left the city a number of groups had been established to pray for the work of the BJS. However, his work in Australia was only just beginning.

9
The Smell of an Oil Rag

I will very gladly spend and be
spent for you… (2 Corinthians 12:15)

Ernest's final destination in Australia was Sydney. Most of his engagements were with the Brethren assemblies, but the Dean of Sydney Cathedral, a firm evangelical with a keen interest in Jewish mission, invited Ernest to preach twice at the Cathedral. Before Ernest left Australia, the Dean presented him with a beautifully inscribed Bible.

Ernest was aware of the existence of the New South Wales Mission to the Jews in Sydney. The Mission consisted of two female members of staff, both Jewish, Miss Gertrude Stargatt and Miss Leah Black. Ernest met the council and assured them that the International Jews Society did not intend to compete with the New South Wales Mission but, instead, wanted to explore the possibility of working with them. The council warmed to him immediately. They arranged an itinerary and invited him to work with them for the duration of his stay.

Gertrude Stargatt, who founded the New South Wales

Mission to the Jews, had been born into a very religious Jewish home in Whitechapel in the East End of London. Through the witness of a Miss Radleigh of the Churches Mission to the Jews, now the Churches Ministry among the Jewish People, Gertrude trusted Jesus as her Saviour and Messiah. As a consequence, her mother refused to speak to her and even when they emigrated to Australia in the nineteen thirties she ignored her completely for the whole of the voyage. On arrival in Sydney, Gertrude was approached by a man who wanted to know if she would consider becoming a missionary to the Jews of the city. He had heard of her coming from the Churches Mission to the Jews in England. With the help of a few others, she founded the New South Wales Mission to the Jews, and for the next fifty years she laboured indefatigably to share the gospel with the Jews of Sydney, supporting herself by the work of her own hands. Her beautiful needlework could have provided her with a more than adequate income, but Gertrude Stargatt chose to concentrate her energies on mission to the Jews, though it meant living in virtual poverty.

Leah Black grew up in a nominally religious home in the north of England in Hull, East Yorkshire. She and her brother and sisters were taught to recite the great Jewish creed, the *Shema* – "Hear, O Israel: the LORD our God is one LORD" – and to observe Sabbath, Passover and the Day of Atonement, but their faith consisted of little more than a mental assent to the major doctrines of Judaism. For many Jewish families, the only religious book in the house is the *Siddur*, the Prayer Book, and Leah had no reason to believe her home was any different until one day she came across a Bible. It had probably found its way into the house through Mr Meadows, a member of the Trafalgar Street Evangelical Church, situated on the Beverley Road, about five minutes walk from the Black home. Meadows visited Leah's father on many occasions, and each time was rebuffed. Yet it was probably his dogged and determined visiting that made it possible for Leah to stumble on the hidden treasure. Another clue that suggests Mr Meadows placed the Bible in the home was the reaction of Leah's sister when she discovered her reading it. She told Leah she was reading "the Christians' Bible". Leah responded that, whoever the Bible belonged to, she was sure it was true.

After the death of their father, Leah, her sisters and brother sold the family home and emigrated to Australia. In Sydney, Leah set up in business and was befriended by a Christian lady, who shared with her that Jesus was the Jewish Messiah who had died for sinners. Leah was astonished when her Gentile friend told her she wished she had been born Jewish because her Saviour was a Jew. Leah was touched by the love her friend and other Christians had for the Jews, but she remained resistant to the claims of Jesus until she heard her friend referring to him as the "sinless Son of God". The phrase triggered some distant memory and the implications of the term struck her. If Jesus was truly the "sinless Son of God", she concluded, to reject him must be the greatest sin of all.

Leah's involvement with Jewish mission came some time later, when the sister who had accused her of reading "the Christian Bible" also became a believer in Jesus and shared with Leah the biblical principle that the gospel is "to the Jew first", from Romans 1:16. Despite being Jewish herself, Leah was reluctant to accept that the Jewish people still had a special place in the purposes of God. Her sister challenged her to think the matter through and, as Leah turned to the Bible, she discovered that not only is the gospel "to the Jew first" but, according to Romans 2:9, so also is judgment. As she continued searching the Scriptures, she discovered that "everything is 'to the Jew first'".

The New South Wales Mission to the Jews conducted a service at their Mission Hall every Sunday afternoon, which Jewish people from varying backgrounds attended. Following her discovery of the principle "to the Jew first", Leah began to help at the Sunday afternoon meeting, an involvement that ultimately led to her becoming the second full-time member of staff.

When he met Gertrude and Leah, Ernest felt a kinship of spirit with them, and they with him. He stayed in Sydney for almost two months and threw himself into their missionary work with alacrity and enthusiasm. Though he and Jessie lived frugally and were devoted to the work of the mission, he was deeply impressed by the dedication and faithfulness of the two ladies who were the New South Wales Mission to the Jews. They lived on very little and Leah cycled dozens of miles each day in summer temperatures of over 100°F to visit her hundreds of Jewish contacts. They called her "the Jewish woman on a bike".

One of her contacts was a brilliant and highly respected rabbi, and Ernest accompanied her to his home. Although the rabbi was unwilling to listen to the gospel, he paid Leah the tribute that, while he did not agree with her beliefs, she was kind and considerate. Another of her contacts was willing to listen to Ernest but, like many Jewish men, he was unwilling to hear a woman speak about religious matters. "You know," he said to Ernest in front of Leah, "we love Leah; she's one of us. But she should go and get married." In Judaism, marriage is important; it is a *mitzvah*, a duty and a meritorious deed for which the righteous will be rewarded in the hereafter. The rabbis teach it is the first *mitzvah* because it was the first biblical commandment, issued to Adam and Eve in Eden. During periods of persecution, when the very existence of the Jewish community seemed in danger, marriage and the begetting of children became increasingly important. Those Jewish communities that have been most exposed to the threat of extinction, such as those in Eastern Europe, still view the begetting of large families as a positive act of righteousness, even though the threat of annihilation has largely passed. In her friend's eyes, Leah had converted to a gentile religion and had forsaken the traditions of her people. In view of the way she was perceived by the rest of the community, it is all the more remarkable that "the woman on a bike" had access to so many Jewish homes.

God blessed Ernest's witness in Sydney, especially through his ministry at the Sunday afternoon meetings held at the mission. The mission hall of the New South Wales Mission to the Jews was, as he wrote in the *Herald* of December 1953, "the only place in Australia where I really felt that I was getting into direct contact with the Jewish people, and where they were prepared to come to a mission to hear the gospel. They were not poor, ignorant Jews; they were Jews of culture, Jews who needed little of this world's goods: but they came because they were interested. It amazed me to find between forty and fifty Jewish people coming along."

At one of the Sunday afternoon services, Ernest spoke about the spiritual need of the Jewish people. The land and material possessions, he told his congregation, could not satisfy Israel's deepest need. After the meeting, a lady approached Ernest full of praise for him and his message. He sensed that she was not a believer in Jesus and that below the effusive surface was "a very needy soul". She had escaped from Warsaw, where her entire family perished in the infamous ghetto, and in Australia she had managed to make a fresh start. She was married to a Jewish watchmaker and they had a beautiful home, but she was deeply dissatisfied. Ernest's Sunday afternoon address struck a chord deep in her heart. When he met her husband, Ernest discovered that he, too, was empty inside. The two of them attended his farewell service and promised to keep in touch.

On his final Saturday in Sydney a group of more than a dozen Jewish children formed an orchestra and performed a concert in his honour. Three of the children were from one family: the older son played the oboe, the younger son the violin, and the girl the piccolo. After the performance, they asked Ernest to make a musical contribution. He sat at the piano and played *Hatikvah*, the anthem of the fledgling state of Israel. When he finished, the mother of the three young musicians was in tears. She had come to the concert only because she wanted to hear her own children play and had made it very clear she would not stay for the evening meeting. Over tea, she told Ernest she would be staying to hear him speak after all.

Ernest's interest in music opened the way for fruitful witness to another of Leah's contacts, a gifted musician. Ernest asked him why it was that most Jewish music was in a minor key. The musician thought the minor key was an appropriate metaphor for human suffering and asked Ernest for his opinion about why the Jewish people had suffered so much. Ernest suggested a number of contributory factors, but the musician wanted to know if he associated Jewish suffering with the death of Jesus. When Ernest said he did, the man accused him of being anti-Semitic. Ernest denied emphatically that he had turned against his own people. The Jewish people bore a responsibility for the death of Jesus, he said, but so did the whole world, because the Messiah died for sinners of all nations. The lengthy discussion that followed was cordial, and in January 1955 Gertrude Stargatt wrote to tell him about the Christmas meeting at the Mission Hall in Sydney:

> You will be overjoyed to know that our Jewish musician
> came and his wife and the children. We got him to play
> and people were just thrilled with his music. Then we
> had a Minister give a very good clear-cut Gospel
> message. Afterwards we had tea and I suddenly looked
> at this man's wife. She was weeping her eyes out! So, I
> went up and said, "I hope no-one has been unkind to
> you." "No, no," she said. "Miss Stargatt, I am sorry to
> give way to my feelings, but you know what really makes
> me weep like this? Everybody in this room loves me."

In Sydney, Ernest discovered that some Anglican churches
had a number of Jewish people in their congregations. St
Paul's in the prestigious Bondi area often had as many as
forty Jewish people at the Sunday evening service. Mrs
Davidson lived in Bondi and was a regular congregant at St
Paul's. She had been born into a religious home and retained
a deep reverence for Orthodox Judaism, but she felt that in
traditional Jewish religion something was missing. For three
years she had been reading the works of Mary Baker Eddy,
the founder of Christian Science, hoping to find answers to
her questions but although she felt the books were wonderful,
they did not answer her deepest need. Ernest counselled her
to forget Mary Baker Eddy and to look at Jesus.

Ernest advised Mrs Davidson to find out more about
Jesus. She could not see that Jesus could help. She saw too
many flaws in Christians, but Ernest persuaded her to read a
book of Jewish testimonies. At Ernest's final meeting in
Sydney, Mrs Davidson confessed that she now believed in
Jesus and was witnessing to others, including her husband.

At the end of 1954, some months after his Australian

tour, he received a letter from a Jewish government official, a man who had been born and brought up in a very Orthodox environment. They had met on a couple of occasions during Ernest's Australian visit, and Ernest felt sure he was not far from the kingdom. In the letter, his Jewish friend shared how "a spiritual revolution" had taken place in his life and that he had just been baptised. He had also written a booklet explaining how the revelation of the Messiah had come to him.

Ernest wrote from Sydney to advise Will Newton of the situation with the New South Wales Mission to the Jews. In his words, the two women were "living on the smell of an oil rag", and he suggested that the two missions work more closely. Newton wrote back to say he had brought the matter to the council and that the BJS was prepared to take the New South Wales Mission under its wing. As a consequence, the pecuniary difficulties of Miss Stargatt and Miss Black were relieved, so much so that Leah was eventually able to travel to her Jewish friends by car instead of on her old sit-up-and-beg pushbike.

A good working relationship developed between the two missions and changes took place in both. In 1971, the New South Wales Mission to the Jews became the Sydney Messianic Fellowship, and in 1976 the British Jews Society and the Barbican Mission to the Jews became Christian Witness to Israel. A serious fall in 1989 severely limited Miss Stargatt's ability to continue her work, and she suggested to CWI's Australia Field Director, John Graham, that the Sydney Messianic Fellowship and CWI merge.

Gertrude Stargatt passed into the presence of her Messiah and Lord on Sunday 23rd August 1992, in her 98th year. Her funeral was well attended and John Graham preached. Leah Black described her as direct, forthright, loyal, down-to-earth, shrewd and an excellent judge of character. To Miss Stargatt, the work of Jewish evangelism was of absolute importance and came before anything else.

Though she was well past retirement age, Leah Black continued the work she and Gertrude Stargatt had begun. Leah's lifestyle was marked by cheerfulness, frugality, generosity and prayer. Each day she prayed for every one of her colleagues in the mission, both in Australia and elsewhere. Until the end, she remained bold in her witness. On a visit to the UK in 1992, when she was taken to a village teashop, she seized the opportunity to share her testimony with everyone.

After she became unable to look after herself at home, Leah spent the last two and a half years of her life in residential care where, though physically weak, she remained strong in faith. She died peacefully in November 2000, aged 89.

10
Land of the Long White Cloud

If any of thine be driven out unto the utmost
parts of heaven, from thence will the LORD
thy God gather thee. (Deuteronomy 30:4)

New Zealand was not so daunting a prospect as Australia.
The principal of the Auckland Bible Institute, John Pritchard,
was a good friend of Ernest. While a Baptist pastor in the UK
at churches in West Croydon and Leigh-on-Sea, Pritchard
had been a firm supporter of the British Jews Society, and in
each of his pastorates he had representatives from the mission
visit every year. Pritchard was on the committee of the
Auckland Missionary Association, and Ernest wrote to ask if
he could arrange a New Zealand itinerary. The Auckland
Missionary Association agreed to arrange a series of
meetings, their only stipulation being that they receive 10%
of any offerings to cover their expenses.

Ernest sailed from Sydney to the Land of the Long White
Cloud, as New Zealand is known in the Maori tongue, on
the Ella. He boarded the boat on Thursday afternoon and
disembarked at Wellington the following Monday morning

at 7 o'clock. A lady met him and presented an itinerary, outlining the arrangements for the whole of his stay in immaculate detail: the trains to ride, the buses to board, the planes to catch and the addresses where he would be staying.

During his first week in New Zealand, he was asked to visit a Jewish lady, Mrs Levy. He agreed but said he hoped that Mrs Levy knew he was a Christian. He found out when he visited her that she didn't. Blanche Levy lived in the gracious Auckland suburb of Parnell, situated on the picturesque Hobson's Bay. When Ernest called, he mentioned the name of the lady who had asked him to visit and Mrs Levy invited him into her home. The conversation was friendly until Ernest told her he was a Hebrew Christian.

"So you think I'm a potential convert?"

He assured Mrs Levy that he was calling on her because he had been asked to, and that he had no ability to convert anyone.

Blanche changed the subject and asked what part of London he came from, and whether he was familiar with the East End.

He told her that he knew the East End of London well and that he had been based in Fournier Street.

"Fournier Street!" Blanche exclaimed. "I was born a minute's walk from Fournier Street! Father and mother were very poor and when we were ill we were taken to the Gilead Medical Mission. But the missionaries never conquered us!"

The barrier between them had been broken down and Blanche invited him to join her and the family on Friday night for their Sabbath meal. He was afraid that the presence of a Hebrew Christian at the meal would be an embarrassment to her. He didn't have to worry, she assured him, the family was under her control.

The Levy family consisted of Blanche, her husband Rueben, their three daughters and one son. Blanche welcomed the Sabbath by lighting the traditional Sabbath candles with the Hebrew blessing, "Blessed art Thou, O Lord our God, King of the Universe, Who hast sanctified us with Thy commandments and commanded us to kindle the light of the holy Sabbath."

Rueben Levy was a quiet man who said little, but the children made it clear they resented Ernest's presence in the home. The eldest daughter asked whether Ernest felt any sense of shame. How could he believe in the Christian religion and be Jewish? It depended on what she meant by "Jewish", he replied. What made *her* Jewish? Was it her faith or the fact that her parents were Jewish? The girl had no answer and became angry, but Blanche interrupted: "Miriam, don't talk to my friend like that! He's not going to convert us."

Blanche wanted to know when Ernest would next be in Auckland so he could visit again. When he returned a month later, Blanche threw her arms round him and welcomed him into the home. She grew to respect Ernest. Religious Jewish families tend to be very closely knit, and Ernest's willingness to be parted from his wife and family for so long out of love for the Messiah earned her admiration. When the time came for him to leave New Zealand, Blanche made Ernest promise to write.

Blanche continued to write to Ernest until her letters suddenly stopped, and he feared the worst. The next time he visited New Zealand, his fears were confirmed. Blanche had died. While clearing up her mother's belongings, Blanche's daughter had come across an envelope addressed to Ernest. He opened it to read Blanche's last letter to him:

My very dear friend,
    My days are numbered but I wanted you to know that I have perfect peace...

Ernest knew what she was saying.

At the behest of the BJS council, Ernest returned every few years to the places where he had established branches of the British Jews Society, in order to encourage the workers and promote the work. New Zealand was different from the other places. In South Africa, Canada and Australia he left behind him workers, but it was not until Ernest's visit to New Zealand in 1960 that R.S. May, a former Warden of the Garden Tomb in Jerusalem, was appointed. May was a conscientious worker and Jewish people became believers through his ministry, but he was elderly and dogged by ill health. It was inevitable that someone younger would have to be recruited if the work in New Zealand was to continue and prosper.

Ernest returned to New Zealand in 1968, this time for the purpose of interviewing a young couple in the South Island, Brian and Vicky Wells. Brian Wells had an unusual story to tell. From his earliest days, he had been taught to fear a God who punished sin, and was told to pray each night for the forgiveness of his transgressions. He was also taught to admire the Jewish people. The family doctor and dentist were both Jewish, and in his teenage years Brian applied to the Council for Relief Services Overseas (CORSO) to work in Israel. His interviewer suggested that the only way to work successfully in Israel would be to go as a missionary and that he should enrol in Bible College.

From Brian's letter of application, it must have been evident to the faculty of the Bible College of New Zealand that Brian was not converted. Nevertheless, they forwarded a prospectus and details of the course, possibly in the hope that the stringent academic requirements would discourage him from pursuing the matter further. If that was the case, they were wrong. Brian's determination to realise his ambition to work in Israel would lead eventually to his conversion.

The Bible College course required him to have some familiarity with New Testament Greek, so Brian and Vicky visited their local library and borrowed everything they could to help them master the language of the New Testament. While studying the Greek text of John's Gospel, Brian made a discovery that would change his life irrevocably. He noticed that in John 1:1 the word "was" ("In the beginning *was* the Word...") differed from "was" in verse 6 ("There *was* a man sent from God..."). Brian saw a deliberate contrast between the Greek verbs *en* in verse 1 and *egeneto* in verses 3, 6 and 18, a contrast that Donald Carson explains in his magisterial commentary on the Fourth Gospel:

> John repeatedly uses the two verbs side by side to establish something of a contrast... In other words, when John uses the two verbs in the same context, *en* frequently signifies existence, whereas *egeneto* signals 'coming into being' or 'coming into use'. In the beginning, the Word was already in existence. Stretch our imagination backward as we will, we can find no point in time where we may agree with Arius, who, speaking of the Word, said, 'There was once when he was not.'

The revelation that Jesus was God led to Brian bowing the knee and receiving him as his Saviour and Lord. That night, for the first time he could remember, Brian did not repeat his childhood prayer for forgiveness. He recalls that he climbed into bed and drifted almost immediately into a deep and peaceful sleep.

Brian's interest in Israel now took on a different complexion. His concern was no longer primarily for the land; he wanted Jewish people to know about salvation through their divine Messiah. A Christian put Brian and Vicky in touch with the International Jews Society and in 1968 Ernest spent a day with them, after which he wrote a lengthy letter to Will Newton recommending their acceptance as missionaries.

Ernest acted as mentor to the Wells and, working alongside him, they gained valuable experience in evangelism and speaking for the mission in churches. Over the years, many Jewish people throughout New Zealand have found the Messiah through the witness of Brian and Vicky. They have developed their own methods of reaching Jewish people of all ages with the gospel, some of which could only work in New Zealand. In what other country would Jewish parents allow their children to attend a youth camp organised by Christians? Through the Bible studies at the camps, Jewish teenagers have discovered Jesus in the Old Testament without ever opening the pages of the New Testament. In the same way, at the *Chaim Hadashim* (New Life) meetings in the Wells' home, Jewish people have found Jesus in the pages of the Hebrew Scriptures. The *Haderekh* (the Way) meetings have helped young Christians to understand the spiritual need of the Jews, while through the *Hatikvah School of Jewish Studies*, Brian and Vicky have nurtured another generation of potential missionaries to the Jewish people.

Through the work of Ernest and Brian and Vicky, a remarkable sequence of events took place that led to the salvation of a number of members of the same family. After speaking at the Presbyterian Church in Dunedin, Ernest was asked if he would visit a Jewish couple, Frank and Fay Sallinger. When Ernest called on them, Frank and Fay welcomed him and they quickly became friends. Ernest sensed that the Spirit of God was at work in their hearts and he visited them almost every day while he was in Dunedin.

Frank had been educated at Clifton School in England,

and was the president of the local synagogue. Though he himself was resistant to the gospel, Frank invited Ernest to speak at his synagogue. Ernest was not sure such a step would be wise; it might cause trouble for Frank. Then would he speak to a group at Frank and Fay's home? Ernest agreed, and a group of twenty turned up for the meeting. Ernest took as his subject, *The Fingerprints of the Messiah,* and began by pointing out that "fingerprints do not lie". He proceeded to expound the messianic passages of the Hebrew Scriptures, arguing that the "fingerprints" of Messiah matched those of Jesus. He covered the entire spectrum of Old Testament prophecy relating to the Messiah: his virgin birth, his birthplace, his crucifixion, his death in the place of sinners and his resurrection from the dead. There followed two and a half hours of questions, most of them aggressive. Fay remained quiet, but after everyone left, she began to ply Ernest with serious questions. After Ernest returned to the UK, Fay wrote to him frequently, asking very serious questions about the faith.

Meanwhile, Brian and Vicky were in contact with a young Jewish couple in Auckland, John and Ruth Sallinger. John was the son of Frank and Fay, and through the witness of Brian and Vicky, he and Ruth both became believers. Although his faith was genuine, John was afraid to tell his parents. He was terrified at what the news might do to them, especially his father. When John and Ruth decided to make *Aliyah* to Israel with their three children, John knew he had to break the news to his parents that not only were he and Ruth going to Israel, but also that they were going as Hebrew Christians. John travelled the 700 miles from Auckland to Dunedin and arrived at the home of his parents early in the morning.

Fay was surprised to see her son and, fearing that something was amiss, asked why he had come. John told her he was emigrating to Israel but that he had something else to tell her which he was afraid would upset her. Before her son could say another word, Fay stopped him. "John, just a moment. I have something to tell *you*. I've become a Christian!"

John and his mother were believers, but God had not finished with the family. Frank and Fay had another son, Peter, living in London, who was married to a religiously observant girl from an ultra-Orthodox background. Fay asked Ernest if there was a Jewish believer in London who could visit Peter. Ernest contacted Richard Harvey, who was then with the Churches Ministry to the Jewish People but is now the lecturer in Jewish studies at All Nations College. Fay's instructions were for Richard to go nowhere near Peter's home but instead to meet Peter at his place of work. Richard made the contact and two years later Peter became a believer in Jesus.

John and his family made *Aliyah* to Israel where today he works alongside David Zeidan, another Jewish believer, distributing Scriptures to kibbutzniks.

11
Ever Increasing Circles

Go ye into all the world, and
preach the gospel... (Mark 16:15)

Ever since the Hebrew Christian Alliance conference of 1934, when Sir Leon Levison spoke of his vision to establish a Hebrew Christian colony in the Holy Land, Ernest had cherished a desire to visit Israel. The February 1955 issue of the *Jewish Missionary Herald*, intimated that Ernest would visit Israel the next month, but in the April issue he reported that during January and February he had been confined to bed with high blood pressure. Nevertheless, he said, he was looking forward to his trip to Israel, but it was as well Ernest had appended D.V. (God willing) to his plans for the following months. A "Stop Press" at the end of the article revealed that illness had prevented him travelling, and the visit would probably take place in September of that year.

That was not to be. A notice in the June issue of the magazine informed readers, "As we go to press we have received a cable from Rhodesia, 'Mr. Katz promoted to glory last night,' and one from Cape Town, 'Mr. Katz with the

Lord'... Please remember Mrs. Katz in this sad and sudden bereavement and also the South Africa staff and those at headquarters who are faced with grave problems by his home-call. We ask your special remembrance of Mr. Lloyd, who will very soon be leaving for Cape Town to help Mr. Levine and Miss Harris."

Three years after his appointment to South Africa, Julius Katz had been found dead on his knees, worn out through his exertions in the cause of Israel's Messiah. Katz suffered from thrombosis and a heart condition and was taken ill during a preaching tour of Rhodesia (Zimbabwe). A heart specialist advised him to return to his wife, but Katz's reply was typical: if he was well enough to return to Cape Town, he was well enough to continue his tour. This stubborn streak no doubt made him difficult to work with, but Eddie Levine was fond of him and wrote in tribute: "Since his coming with Mrs. Katz to the union of South Africa he has travelled thousands of miles, bringing the Word of Redeeming Grace to Jewish homes, shops, synagogues and hospitals... His last trophy of Grace, which he termed 'the first-fruits of the Rhodesian tour', was a young Jewess of nineteen years of age whom he led to Christ as the train was entering the Rhodesian border."

Ernest believed Katz had had a premonition of his impending death, which was why he refused to slow down in the work. In a letter to Ernest, written shortly before he died, Katz wrote: "Here we are overworking. But, thank God, Jesus is stronger than Satan and sin. We must realise, dear Ernest, that this truth has to be learned."

Ernest arrived in Cape Town on 19th July, the middle of the South African winter. In a rare allusion to his feelings, he wrote in the BJS magazine: "Here I am writing from 'Sunny South Africa', only it happens to be winter here and quite cold! How I would love to be with my wife and the boys on holiday in Scotland! But God has work for me to do here and I must do it well". His first meeting was the next day, and three days later he was in Port Elizabeth, 500 miles east of Cape Town. From there he travelled to other towns and cities, returning to Cape Town for a fortnight's meetings before travelling back to the UK on 7th October. It was a gruelling itinerary, not least because from 11th August until the time of his departure two months later, he did not have one day free.

Ernest was deeply moved by the evident drift away from Judaism that he observed wherever he went. Traditional Jewish religion left its followers empty. In a Johannesburg hotel lobby, the elderly widow of a rabbi confided that since her husband had died, she had nothing. She had clung to Jewish tradition all her life and now she was old and disillusioned with it all.

Preaching at a crowded Brethren hall one Sunday evening, Ernest noticed a young Jewish couple sitting in the front row. They had come out of curiosity after seeing the meeting advertised in a local paper. The couple did not agree with what he had said that evening but they could understand what he was saying, whereas at the synagogue services they could understand nothing. They asked if Ernest would join them and another Jewish couple for a meal, and he agreed. They were intelligent, cultured and, as Ernest discovered when he arrived at their beautiful home, very wealthy. It was the time of the festival of Sukkot, or Tabernacles, and they proudly showed him the beautifully decorated booth they had erected in the garden. They confided in Ernest that they observed Judaism out of respect for their parents, but after their parents were dead, they would feel no compunction in turning their backs on Jewish religion. They had been fascinated by the fact that in his preaching Ernest had not mentioned "religion" and that in almost every other sentence he spoke of "Jesus". He pointed out that this was the great difference between his faith and theirs. They were clinging to a dead religion; he had a personal faith in a living Saviour. Far from being offended by his straight talk, the four young Jewish people wanted to talk to him again.

In Johannesburg, Ernest was invited to address the students of the Medical Faculty of the University, accompanied by Eddie Levine. Just as he and Eddie were about to enter the auditorium, they were told that the evening newspaper had queered the pitch for them. Ernest had consented to an interview with the papers but the reporter had so distorted his statements that the Jewish students were infuriated and intent on venting their wrath. As he entered the auditorium, the sense of anger was palpable, and Ernest knew he had to turn the situation around. To these irate young Jews he was an interferer, and he had somehow to take the wind out of their sails. In dependence on God, he chose to speak on "The Divine Interference", proving from the Old Testament how the Almighty had continually interfered in the affairs of Israel and that the Jewish people did not like it. The advent of Messiah, he told his audience, was God's ultimate intervention in the history of Israel and the gospel itself is a divine interference in the affairs of mankind.

Not a sound was heard while Ernest spoke, and as he concluded his talk the audience remained silent. He opened the meeting to the floor and fielded questions. In the comments and objections he detected the same sense of spiritual frustration and lassitude that he found everywhere else. After the meeting, the son of a rabbi approached him to say that he had come to the event to pull Ernest to pieces but, after listening to him, he felt as though he himself had been pulled to pieces.

During his four months in South Africa, Ernest not only defended the faith but also led a number into the faith. After preaching at a Sunday morning service in a Methodist church, a Jewish man in his early twenties thanked him for the sermon and asked if he might talk to him further. The following day, the young man arrived at the Baptist manse where Ernest was staying. Ernest's message the previous morning had helped him to see that Jesus was the Messiah and that salvation was by God's grace alone. It was evident that the young man was not far from the kingdom, and before he left the manse he received Jesus as his Saviour.

A week later, in a city some 250 miles away, Ernest was staying at the home of a Methodist minister. He had only just arrived at the manse when a Hebrew Christian from the town where Ernest had led the young Jew to the Lord called to ask if Mr Lloyd was staying there. In the conversation that followed, he shared with Ernest that he had been a believer for three years, the only one in his family, so he thought. The previous week he had received a letter from his brother in Mafeking to say that he also had found Jesus. Ernest rejoiced with him and then related the story of the young Jew who had come to the Messiah in the man's own town. When he heard the young man's name, the Hebrew Christian was ecstatic; it was his nephew. There were now three believers in the family.

On his only Sunday in Johannesburg, Ernest spoke at a Youth for Christ evangelistic rally in the Classic cinema. The cinema was full for the event and over forty responded to the altar call, including a Jew and a Roman Catholic. For over an hour, Ernest and Eddie Levine counselled the Jewish man and knelt with him on the floor of the cinema where he acknowledged Jesus as his Redeemer.

*****

From 1951 to the time of his retirement in 1978, there were only six years when Ernest was not overseas on behalf of the mission, and he was never away for less than three months at a time. In the year following his emergency visit to South Africa, his travels were confined to the British Isles, but in March 1957, *The Editor's Memoranda* column in the BJS *Jewish Missionary Herald* recorded that "Mr. Lloyd is fulfilling as many engagements as possible before flying to New Zealand". The year began with a deputation tour of Cornwall, followed by meetings in Stockport in Cheshire, Hitchin in Hertfordshire, March and Chatteris in Cambridgeshire and Dublin in the Irish Republic, before returning to England for meetings in Henley-on-Thames and Bedford. He recorded in the *Herald*, "I was so knocked out by the various inoculations I had to have, I had most regretfully to cancel my engagements in Letchworth". Once recovered, however, he embarked on a deputation tour of Somerset and Devon.

Ernest left London on 8th April 1957 and returned on 8th October. The tour took him to India, Ceylon, Singapore, Australia, Tasmania, New Zealand and, for the first time, Canada. The editor's comment that the tour would be "an arduous undertaking" was an understatement. The media speak of the "gruelling schedules" of campaigning politicians in the weeks leading up to a general election, or of the Roman pontiff on his pastoral forays outside the walls of the Vatican, but none of those schedules compare with Ernest's itinerary during those six months in 1957. He flew a total of 46,000 miles and spoke at 279 meetings – an average of almost 2,000 miles and ten meetings every week!

He left Heathrow on a cold spring morning and stepped off the plane in a Bombay that was suffering a heatwave. Even the locals were wilting, and Ernest was soon longing for the cold of England. John Buffam met him and informed him that he had many meetings arranged. One of his first engagements was at the Queen Mary High School for Girls, which was run by the Zenana Bible and Medical Mission. Half the girls in his audience were Jewish with the other half fairly evenly divided into Moslems and Hindus. There were also three Jewish teachers. Ernest spoke about missionary work and the history of Israel, after which he was asked questions. He had been allotted an hour, but the questions came thick and fast and he was there for two and a half hours: What did it mean to be "converted"? Could he "prove" the Trinity? Where was Jesus in the Old Testament? At the end of the session, some of the Jewish girls and two of the teachers approached him to ask if he was speaking anywhere else, and on each of the three nights he was in Bombay they turned up at his meetings.

Only one of his meetings during the three days he spent in Bombay was for Christians. The rest were primarily evangelistic, and at each one some fifty to sixty Jewish people gathered. After each event there was opportunity for questions and discussion, and a lively exchange invariably ensued.

On the Sabbath, Ernest accompanied John Buffam to the home of the rabbi, on the third storey of a dilapidated tenement building where the smell from the open sewers and putrefying refuse in the street was suffocating. They were greeted warmly by their host and his fifteen children. After bowing politely to their guests, his children took their places on the floor around their father, who sat crossed-legged on a bed. The dark skinned figure was typically Indian but his speech and manners were thoroughly Jewish. After talking for a while, the rabbi asked if Ernest had any questions. Ernest asked if the rabbi had ever read the fifty-third chapter of Isaiah. The man confessed that he had not. Had he a copy of the Hebrew Scriptures? He said he had. The oldest son was sent to bring it and the whole company, including the rabbi and Ernest, read it aloud. The rabbi judged the chapter to be very beautiful, but Ernest wanted to know of whom the prophet spoke. Who was the righteous Servant of the Lord on whom "the iniquity of us all" was laid? The rabbi said he would need to look at his rabbinic commentaries. Ernest assured him that there was no need to consult the opinions of rabbis; the passage was about the Messiah, the Redeemer of Israel. The entire morning was spent talking about the Messiah and as Ernest and John rose to leave, the rabbi asked when he would next be in Bombay so they could continue their discussion.

In Ceylon, now Sri Lanka, Ernest spoke to five hundred young Sinhalese Christians at a Bible camp. It was a time when nationalistic and anti-British feelings were running high. The country had been an independent nation for almost ten years, and when S.W.R.D. Bandaranaike became Prime Minister in 1956, his government passed a law that made Sinhalese the country's only official language, an action the Tamils resented, and clashes broke out between Tamils and Sinhalese. The Prime Minister then provoked the anger of his fellow Sinhalese by compromising with the Tamils. In the BJS *Herald*, Ernest expressed his opinion that "the time is not far distant when English people will have to leave Ceylon". He was concerned, therefore, that the Sinhalese church should be made aware of their spiritual obligation to the Jewish people, and during his short time there a number of the young people thanked him for making them aware of their debt to the Jews. Two years later, in 1959, a Sinhalese extremist assassinated Solomon Bandaranaike and the country has remained in the grip of terror from both Tamil and Sinhalese radicals ever since.

*****

After a brief stopover in Singapore, Ernest arrived in Sydney, where he again worked closely with the New South Wales Mission to the Jews. A local radio station invited him to broadcast eight half hour talks on the subject of "Redemption in the Old Testament". Wisely, he chose not to target Jewish listeners but, instead, aimed his talks at "all those who had not experienced redemption", occasionally illustrating his point in a way that would strike a chord with Jewish listeners. Some Christians felt he should have preached directly to the Jewish people, but Ernest knew that if any of his listeners felt they were being "got at" they would simply switch off the radio and he would lose them. After the third broadcast, one of the announcers handed Ernest a letter from a Jewish businesswoman, asking if she could meet him in her lunch hour. She was conscious of a spiritual vacuum in her life and Ernest's broadcast talks had made a deep impression on her. Before Ernest left the city the young woman had experienced redemption. Her husband was angry, but he could not deny the change that had taken place in his wife and the evident sense of peace she enjoyed.

In New Zealand, Ernest received a telephone call from a man who said only that he was a Jew and wanted to meet him without a Christian present. The man had been raised in an Orthodox Jewish home and was married to a Jewish woman. After careful consideration, they had decided to send their children to a Christian Sunday School rather than to the Jewish equivalent, the *Heder*. Their decision had angered their rabbi, who accused the couple of being Christians, an accusation the man denied. He had started to read the New Testament and discovered that instead of negating the ancient faith of Israel, it substantiated it. He and Ernest met on four other occasions. The man was not totally convinced of the case for Jesus, but at their final meeting he said, "Mr Lloyd, it is not that I do not want to be convinced. But I will never become a Christian unless I can be an honest Christian, and until I can really and truly say, 'Thou art indeed the Christ, the Son of the living God'."

The visit to New Zealand also resulted in a step forward for the mission. Before Ernest left, Hugh Saunderson had been appointed the BJS national representative.

*****

Ernest's first visit to Canada was with the intention of making the work of the BJS more widely known, to evangelise and to explore the possibilities for starting a work there. Will Newton had visited Vancouver soon after becoming the General Secretary of the BJS. There were a number of Hebrew Christians in the city, and Newton had recognised the potential for a Canadian branch of the mission. Ernest arrived in Vancouver, where a busy programme of meetings had been prepared, after which he moved on to Montreal and Winnipeg.

The Jewish population of Montreal at that time numbered 136,000, the largest concentration of Jews in North America after New York. Today, 100,000 Jews live in the city, with larger numbers in Miami, Los Angeles, Philadelphia, Chicago, San Francisco and Boston. In the seven years prior to his visit, five synagogues had been built, but Ernest was appalled to discover that, with one exception, no Christians in Montreal were attempting to reach the burgeoning Jewish community with the gospel. One Christian lady was evangelising the Jewish people of Montreal, and she invited Ernest to visit some of her Jewish contacts, among whom was the widow of a rabbi. They called just before New Year and Ernest was introduced as a Hebrew Christian. She told him he was *meshuganeh*, but he reminded her that in a short time it would be *Yom Kippur*, the Day of Atonement: did she know her sins were gone? She confided that the thought of death terrified her and that she had no hope beyond this life.

In Winnipeg, while eating lunch with friends at a Jewish Youth Club, Ernest became aware that he was attracting the attention of a group of Jewish young people. Two of the group came over to his table and asked if he was talking about Christianity. The conversation resulted in a meeting that very afternoon with the rabbi responsible for Jewish youth work. At the end of their discussion, the rabbi said that if he believed Jesus was the Messiah of his people, he would go to the highest building in the city, and shout it to the whole of Winnipeg.

A representative of the American Association for Jewish Evangelism was based in Winnipeg, Hebrew Christian Harry Flumbaum. Harry and Ernest had much in common and they became friends immediately. Both were married to gentiles and both had a single purpose in life – to win Jewish people for the Saviour. On a return visit to Canada the following year, Ernest spent Christmas with Harry and his wife. The Wednesday after the festival, Harry announced that he was taking Ernest to see a rabbi. The rabbi, a young Romanian Jew, was obviously delighted to see Harry and Ernest. He gave them both a warm welcome and then, to Ernest's amusement, asked if Harry had had a good Christmas.

Harry had. Did the rabbi have a good Hanukkah? The rabbi said he did.

"Who's this man?" the rabbi asked.

"One of us," said Harry.

"Does he believe like you do?"

"Yes."

"I'll see if I can demolish him."

Harry laughed. "You haven't demolished me yet."

"Oh, you're a stubborn Jew!"

In the discussion that followed the rabbi quoted the sages of Israel to support his viewpoint. Ernest tried without success to get the rabbi to hear what the Tanakh, the Old Testament, had to say about the issues they addressed.

"We don't understand half of the Tanakh," said the young rabbi. He preferred the sayings of the rabbis and thought it was tragic that Jesus changed his religion. Ernest asked what religion he thought Jesus had been brought up in.

"He was kosher."

"And he *remained* kosher, Rabbi."

"I told Harry that Jesus invented a new religion."

Ernest suggested that if the rabbi would read the New Testament without prejudice, he would see that Jesus said he did not come to destroy the Torah, he came to fulfil it. The rabbi thought both men were mistaken. Harry Flumbaum responded candidly: "No Rabbi, it's you that's mistaken. Why do you want to bother with all the Talmudic teaching? The Talmud has some wonderful teaching but it also has some very naive folklore."

Ernest and Harry arrived at the rabbi's house at one thirty in the afternoon and left at nine thirty in the evening, having made little apparent progress. The incident serves to correct the popular misconception that Judaism has remained unchanged since biblical times and that the Bible alone is the basis of Jewish religious thought. Judaism today bears little resemblance to the religion of Moses and the prophets. To understand the changes in Jewish religious thought, we have to understand the significance of events that occurred in the year 70 AD.

In biblical times, Judaism revolved around the sacrificial system, and until its destruction at the hands of the Romans in 70 AD, the temple was the hub of Jewish life. Without the temple, the sacrificial system could no longer continue; without the sacrifices, the priesthood could no longer function; without the temple, the sacrifices and the priesthood, the Jewish faith could no longer exist in the form revealed to Moses. The Sadducees, the temple aristocracy, fell from power, and into the vacuum created by the disappearance of the temple stepped the Pharisees. The great architect of post-biblical Judaism was Rabbi Johanan ben Zakkai, a Pharisee who, on the basis of Psalm 51:17 – "The sacrifices of God are a broken spirit" – ruled that sacrifice was not a prerequisite for divine forgiveness. It is recorded that on one occasion, as Rabbi Johanan and his disciple Rabbi Joshua looked on the ruins of the temple, Rabbi Joshua cried out, "Woe is us; the place where Israel obtained atonement for sins is in ruins." Rabbi Johanan reassured him, "My son, be not distressed. We still have an atonement equally efficacious, and that is the practice of benevolence."

The "traditions of the fathers" which Christ challenged constituted a significant departure from revealed truth, and with the dissolution of the temple came the demise of a Judaism based on the Torah alone; rabbinic tradition reigned. When Rabbi Johanan ruled that sacrifice was no longer necessary for forgiveness, he added another stone to the foundation of a system that would ultimately place the word of the rabbis above the Word of God. The influential *Pirke Avot* – Sayings of the Fathers – states that "Moses received the Law from Sinai and committed it to Joshua, and Joshua to the elders..." The "Law" that the *Pirke Avot* refers to is not the Ten Commandments but the "Oral Tradition", an unwritten explanation of the meaning of the written Law. There is, of course, no biblical evidence for the claim that two laws – one written and the other oral – were delivered to Moses at Sinai. Nevertheless, belief in the divine origin of the "Oral

Law" has persisted to this day. The *Talmud*, which is the oral tradition in written form, has in practice usurped the authority of Scripture. When we understand this, we understand why the Romanian rabbi was reluctant to base his beliefs on Scripture alone.

It would be another eleven years before the mission was able to place a full-time worker in Vancouver, and Ernest was to return to Canada three times before that, including a nine month period in which he and Jessie helped to establish and strengthen the work of the mission. In all, he visited Canada eight times in the next twenty years, spending a total of more than two and a half years in the country. Vancouver would also be the final destination of a marathon nine month tour undertaken just before his retirement in 1978.

12
Promised Land

View the land.... (Joshua 2:1)

To travel to the Holy Land on an El Al jet with a contingent of Orthodox Jews is quite an experience. When the plane touches down, a wave of joyful excitement sweeps through the plane. Four eventful years after he had first been scheduled to visit Israel, in 1958 Ernest finally fulfilled his ambition. As he stepped off the plane onto Israeli soil, he did so with a sense of gratitude to God and the mission for the privilege of being allowed to go to the land of his ancestors. However, he felt no sense of exuberance. Ernest harboured no sentimental attachment to the land of Israel; he had always believed that people were more important than places.

Ernest was welcomed to *Eretz Yisrael* by Dr J.C. Churcher and his wife, who drove him to the BJS headquarters in Haifa. The medical mission on the slopes of Mount Carmel in Haifa was the hub of the BJS work in Israel. It dated back to 1920, when A.P. Gold-Levin and A.Y. Nisset arrived from England to establish the *Mount Carmel Bible School for Earnest Seekers after Truth* and to provide medical aid in premises that had been donated by D.C Joseph, a Polish Jewish Christian.

Joseph had come to faith in the Messiah on the Isle of Man in 1860, and for the next 25 years witnessed to Jews in the East End of London. In the 1880s, he moved to Jerusalem, where he led Sabbati Benjamin Rohold to the Messiah. Rohold was the son of a *shochet*, a ritual slaughterer, and would later become a major figure in the world wide Hebrew Christian Alliance. After he became a believer in Jesus, he found his life in danger and had to flee to England, where he studied for the Anglican ministry. Rohold returned to Palestine in 1919 as an ordained Church of England minister, and suggested that Joseph entrust a property he had purchased in Haifa to the BJS.

Five years later, Dr James Churcher arrived in Haifa. He had given up a promising medical career in England, and for the next 53 years, until his retirement in 1977, he served the Jewish and Arab communities in Haifa sacrificially and without reserve. His father had been the physician at the BJS medical mission in Whitechapel, and James himself had had some experience at the mission at times when his father was ill. When he arrived in Haifa there was a Reading Room, a Bible shop and a medical dispensary equipped with the most primitive of facilities. Gospel meetings, Bible classes and language lessons were well attended, and the young doctor was soon in great demand. Every morning before 8.30am, upwards of a hundred patients were lined up on the long benches in the waiting room. Between 1924 and 1931 the population of Haifa trebled, and the staff could not deal with the numbers who came seeking medical help, and many had to be turned away. Churcher's marriage to Gladys Naylor in 1935 provided the medical mission with a receptionist, pharmacist, assistant nurse and general helper!

European Jews fleeing the terror of Nazism during the thirties and forties intensified the need for medical care in Haifa. In the spring and summer of 1941, thousands flocked to the clinic, and in July of that year alone the mission treated over 2,000 people. Gospel meetings were well attended and one man, attracted initially by the sound of hymn singing from the Reading Room, subsequently confessed Jesus as his Saviour. After the Second World War, hatred between Arabs and Jews heightened. The Grand Mufti of Jerusalem had openly supported Hitler, and many Arabs had hoped that the German Führer would succeed in his plan to exterminate European Jewry. Jewish patients were treated at the Hadar clinic in the town centre, while Arabs were looked after at the Mount Carmel premises. Life became increasingly dangerous so that in 1947 British members of staff were ordered to leave Haifa. In spite of the danger, Dr Churcher decided to remain in the city.

During those dangerous days, when the city was under curfew, Dr Churcher received a call from the English High School, where the Arab cook was seriously ill. In spite of the risk involved, the doctor answered the call without hesitation but after attending to the cook he had "a strong presentiment" that he should not return by way of the Jewish quarter. Some months later an Arab patient informed him that he was "lucky" not to have been killed that night. On the evening in question, the patient had been alongside a hidden Arab sniper. The gunman had wanted to shoot the doctor but his companion protested. The sniper agreed to spare the doctor only if he went back the same way he had come; if Dr Churcher went in the direction of the Jewish quarter he would kill him.

In April 1948, British staff returned to Haifa, and one month later, on 14th May 1948, Dr Churcher and his staff witnessed the British High Commissioner sail out of Haifa

Bay and Israel declare itself an independent state.

James Churcher was not only a first-rate physician; he was first and foremost an evangelist. Because he did not speak Ivrit, Ernest did little direct evangelism during the month he was in Israel, but he had abundant opportunity to witness Dr Churcher the evangelist in action. He lost no opportunity to speak of Jesus, whether in the surgery or on the rare occasions when he was off-duty. Ernest was present in the consulting room when the doctor examined a young Israeli suffering from a skin complaint. Before sending him to get his medicine, the doctor quietly explained to him his need of the Saviour and handed him a gospel pamphlet.

Dr and Mrs Churcher drove Ernest the length and breadth of the land of the Bible, visiting sites with names familiar from the pages of Scripture: Jezreel, Galilee, Capernaum, Cana and Nazareth. Churcher never missed an opportunity to witness. Every hitchhiker was a soul in need of the gospel. The doctor would stop the car: "Where are you going?"

"Bethlehem."

"I'm going that way. Get in."

A conversation would ensue immediately. Hikers usually wanted to know who the doctor was and what had brought him to Israel. He would tell them of his great esteem for the nation and how his father had taught his eight children to respect the Jewish people. That prepared the way for talking about the gospel.

Driving south to Beersheba, they gave a lift to a Jewish girl, a native-born Sabra. As far as she was concerned, Ernest was not a true Jew because he had not been born in the land. He reminded her that they were both descended from their father Abraham but she was adamant, only those born in the land were true Jews. The conversation showed Ernest that although the new state was only a decade old, cracks in the fabric of Israeli society were already apparent. Jews from so many lands and cultures, speaking different languages and holding widely diverse customs, were converging on a piece of Middle East real estate, no bigger than Wales, and trying to live together.

Two other girls were curious about Ernest. Who was he? How could he be Jewish and a Christian? Dr Churcher asked them to define "Jewishness"; was it a matter of religion or race? The girls were Jewish, but apart from observing the rituals of Yom Kippur each year, they had little interest in religion. For them, Jewishness was a matter of ethnicity. Was it the same with Christians? Churcher explained that neither he nor Ernest were born Christians. Although Ernest was a Jew and the doctor was a gentile, they each had been born in sin and needed a Redeemer.

Dr Churcher's fame spread throughout Israel, earning him the respect of both Jews and Arabs, and he was affectionately nicknamed "Dr Churchill". In 1937, Dr Churcher was honoured with the King's Medal and, following his retirement in 1977, the Queen awarded him the OBE for his services to the people of Israel. Checking in at the airport on his departure from Israel, Ernest was asked who he was and where he had been staying. When he mentioned the name of Dr Churcher, his interrogator's face brightened. The doctor had helped the man's wife: "Dr Churcher is a wonderful man," he said. "He is not only a medical man, he is such a friend to our people."

The crowning glory of Dr Churcher's ministry in Haifa was revealed on his last day at the mission before his retirement. He and his wife were writing labels for their cases when a Tunisian Jewess, whom the doctor had treated in the past for a leg problem, appeared. Churcher was busy but he put aside his labels and asked what he could do for her. She replied that she did not require medical help; she wanted to become a Christian. Dr Churcher explained to her what it meant to believe in Jesus and when he had finished, she quietly submitted her life to the Messiah.

*****

The beauty of Haifa is stunning. The mission headquarters were built on the slopes of Mount Carmel – the "Vineyard of the Lord", now the site of Israel's largest national park, covering an area of about 21,000 acres – overlooking Haifa Bay. The above average rainfall, the climate, geographical structure and the soil combine to ensure the area is green all the year round, making Haifa and Mount Carmel one of the most beautiful spots in the whole of Israel. A common flower on Mount Carmel is the cyclamen – *rakefes* in Hebrew – the shape of which resembles a small crown. Unlike other flowers that face toward the sky, the *rakefes* bends toward the ground and the people of Haifa say it is waiting until Messiah comes to restore the crown of glory to Israel. Then the *rakefes* will lift its crowned head proudly to heaven.

On his first Friday evening in Haifa, as Ernest leaned over the balcony of the mission house, he remarked to Dr Churcher that there were not so many neon lights visible that night. It was Shabbat and although the young state of Israel was in many ways godless, even a secular city such as Haifa observed the day of rest. The observance of the Sabbath was impressive but it could also be inconvenient, as Ernest and the Churchers discovered after a trip to Eilat in the south. The plane bringing them back from Eilat landed at Lod on Friday evening after Shabbat had begun, and all public transport and taxis had ceased operating until the next evening. Dr Churcher was unperturbed. "A walk won't do you any harm!" he said, and together they set off to walk the sixteen miles to Lydda, helped on their way only when an Arab with a very weary looking donkey came along and allowed them to take turns riding the poor animal.

The dedication of the Haifa staff impressed Ernest far more than the beauty of the city and its surroundings. The mission had been established for one great purpose – to take Messiah to Israel – and the staff gave themselves totally to accomplish that aim. They worked all day, every day with hardly any rest. Patients arrived early, and before breakfast the doctor and nurses were caring for the sick. When surgery was over Elizabeth Wyatt, Ida Draitschman, Dorothea Marx and Mrs Kinder visited patients in their homes. Haifa was a modern city with blocks of flats, but many of those in need of medical attention lived in small, airless huts that became unbearably hot in summer.

Another helper in Haifa was Huguette Harari, a vivacious Egyptian Jewess who had been a help to Eddie Levine after he came to faith. Her French Bible studies attracted good numbers and when Ernest was present some forty young people, most of them married couples, were there. One of the young women told how the previous week's study had cleared up a number of difficulties for her. The meeting lasted for at least two and a quarter hours, and afterwards three of the young couples stayed to talk further.

As an officer of the Hebrew Christian Alliance, Ernest was keen to meet other Hebrew Christians. Unlike today, Jewish believers in Israel were few and scattered, and were afraid to be open about their faith. A father of three asked how he could make an open confession of his faith in Jesus, when it would mean that his wife and children would suffer and he would lose his job.

Apart from leading a tour of Israel and attending the

Jubilee Conference of the International Hebrew Christian Alliance in Jerusalem in 1974, Ernest's association with the land has been minimal. Some may find it hard to believe that such a major figure in the Messianic Jewish world should have spent so little time in the Holy Land but, as Ernest has always maintained, people are more important than places and souls more precious than land.

13
Bread on the Waters

Who hath believed our report? (Isaiah 53:1)

Early in 1955, following discussions with G.H. Howlett of the Old Mission Church Hebrew Mission in Calcutta, the BJS "entered into a fraternal and practical co-operation with him and his fellow workers". Although the Jewish population of India was declining in the wake of India's independence in 1947 and the establishment of the state of Israel the following year, there were still some 1,500 Jews living in Calcutta. As a consequence of the formal association with the Old Mission Church, the BJS contributed to the training and support of Richard Bowie, Howlett's assistant evangelist.

Ernest had visited India and Ceylon briefly in 1953 and 1957. In 1963, he returned with the intention of staying longer, but on arrival in Calcutta, it appeared he was not going to be allowed into the country. The immigration authorities had never encountered a "missionary to the Jews" before, and Ernest was questioned at length about the purpose of his visit before being informed that the Indian government would not allow him to speak at any public meetings. Ernest persisted with his request to enter the country as a missionary and to be able to address a series of meetings. In the end, his exasperated interrogator instructed him to write a letter to the Chief of Police informing him of the purpose of his visit and what he proposed to do in India. The letter was scrawled on the only scrap of paper he could find and he was allowed into the country. Once through customs, Richard Bowie escorted him to the Old Mission Church.

Bowie was anxious to use Ernest to the full and wanted him to visit as many Jewish homes as possible during the time he was in Calcutta. Before Ernest had time to unpack, Bowie was ready to introduce him to Jewish friends. Their first call was to a Jewish mother and her two grown-up sons, who showed the two missionaries typical Indian hospitality. She prepared coffee and, as her guests seated themselves, she asked Ernest why he had left such a wonderful faith as Judaism with its many beautiful traditions. Ernest answered that he had not forsaken Judaism. Instead, in Jesus, he had found the fulfilment of the Jewish faith. She asked if he observed Passover. He told her that he didn't. Did he fast on Yom Kippur? He had no need to fast on the Day of Atonement because the blood of Messiah had atoned for his sins, once and for all. He shared with her that Jesus was a Jew who said he did not come to destroy the Law, but to fulfil it. The lady was fascinated by his answer. She had thought missionaries undermined the religion of Israel, but Ernest was able to assure her that this was not so. She invited them to stay for a meal so they could continue the discussion. During his two weeks in Calcutta, he and Richard Bowie visited many Jewish homes, and in each one they were able to disabuse Jewish people of their misconceptions about the gospel and point them to the Messiah.

Ernest delivered a series of talks on Jewish evangelism at

the Old Mission Church. As he began his first lecture, a very tall, handsome gentleman, resplendent in beautiful purple robes entered. It was evident that he was a dignitary in the church but, beyond that, Ernest had no idea who the man was. Archbishop Demell was, in fact, the Metropolitan Bishop for the whole of India and Ceylon and he later phoned to request that Ernest visit him. When Ernest arrived at the bishop's palace, some forty other people were waiting to see the bishop and he took his place at the end of the line. Minutes later a chaplain appeared to ask if Mr Lloyd from England was there. Ernest identified himself and was immediately escorted into the office of the Metropolitan. Ernest felt uncomfortable in the presence of the church dignitary, but the bishop put him at his ease. He thanked Ernest for the talk he had given and confessed that, until he heard his lecture, he had no idea that anyone was trying to "Christianise Jews". It was, he admitted, an area of mission that the Church had neglected. He showed great interest in Ernest and asked where he would be going after leaving India. On learning that he would be in Ceylon, Archbishop Demell enquired whether he had meetings arranged there. Ernest explained that the Bishop of Colombo had forbidden him to speak in any of his pulpits. The Metropolitan rang for his secretary and immediately dictated a letter authorising "Mr Ernest Lloyd of the British Jews Society" to occupy any Anglican pulpit in Ceylon. Before Ernest left, the Metropolitan prayed with him that God would show mercy to the nation of Israel and bring the Jewish people to faith in their Messiah.

Ernest returned elated to the Old Mission House where, to his utter astonishment, he found the Bishop of Colombo. Unlike his superior, the bishop was pompous and haughty. When he and Ernest were introduced, the bishop informed him, in a plummy English accent, that he knew of him and was afraid he could not permit him to speak in any of the churches in Ceylon. Ernest handed him the freshly written letter and the man blanched as he read it. "This is from the Metropolitan?" he asked. Suppressing a gleeful smile, Ernest informed the deflated bishop that the Metropolitan of India and Ceylon had attended one of his meetings and that he had just returned from an audience with him.

Arriving in Ceylon, Ernest was warmly greeted by a high ranking civil servant who was also the local president of the British and Foreign Bible Society. Ernest had been seeking openings into the Anglican churches on the island, and the Metropolitan's letter was all he needed. At one meeting, some 25 Anglican ministers, resplendent in their clerical attire, were present.

A young Jew from the Canadian Embassy in Colombo invited Ernest to his home for Sunday lunch. Ernest arrived promptly at noon and was immediately bombarded with questions by the educated young Jew: Why did he leave Judaism? What is a Christian? How could he be both a Jew and a Christian? It was almost five o'clock before everyone sat down to lunch. The lady of the house had a widowed mother in Winnipeg, Ontario, where Ernest was due later on in his itinerary. Ernest asked that when the young woman next wrote to her mother, she mention him and what they had been talking about. He told Harry Flumbaum of the contact and a few weeks later received a letter from Harry telling him that he had visited the widow and received a very warm reception.

*****

In 1963, the BJS magazine the *Herald* changed to a smaller format, and inside the back cover, under the heading, *Our*

Field the World, there regularly appeared a list of the international branches and workers. For more than ten years, thanks to God's blessing on the sacrificial efforts of Ernest, the BJS had been expanding its ministry beyond the shores of the UK. To reflect the mission's broader ministry, in 1965 the British Jews Society became the International Society for the Evangelization of the Jews. The overseas expansion of the work would continue that year also, with the addition of a Canadian branch.

The Bible Testimony Fellowship, a mission to the Jews in Vancouver in British Columbia, had existed for a number of years. The BTF consisted of three ladies – Miss Doris Profitt, Miss Florence Seally and Miss Florence Edge – and in 1964 the ladies proposed that the IJS take over the work of the Bible Testimony Fellowship. On Ernest's world tour of 1965, Vancouver was included in the itinerary. There was a comfortable mission house in Osler Street, and the following year he and Jessie returned for a nine-month stay, based in the mission house.

Although Ernest's position in the mission since 1959 had been Overseas Deputation Secretary, he remained first and foremost a missionary. The IJS intended that his 1966/67 visit would be to speak in churches and raise the profile of the work, but he and Jessie were also determined to use the mission house as a base for outreach to the Vancouver Jewish community. They commenced a meeting for Jewish people at the house in Osler Street and Ernest began visiting Jewish homes to make the meeting known.

The Vancouver Jewish community was reasonably affluent, and few of those on whom Ernest called wished their comfortable lifestyles to be disturbed. Door after door was closed in his face, but he persevered until a nucleus of Jewish people, including a lady doctor, began to meet to study the Bible. Ernest appealed for prayer at the churches he visited but requested Christians not to attend the meetings. Some felt offended that they should be excluded from the gatherings, but the wisdom of his strategy became all too evident when a zealous but misguided Christian lady gatecrashed one of the studies. Ernest was incensed when he overheard the woman inform the doctor that her people had crucified Jesus. The doctor, visibly distressed at being labelled a "Christ killer", rose to leave but Ernest persuaded her to stay. He ordered the Christian lady out of the house and instructed her never to return.

Jewish people are keenly aware that throughout the Middle Ages they were persecuted by the Church as "Christ killers". Therefore, "Christ", "cross" and "conversion" still resonate negatively in the psyche and emotions of Jewish people. There are Jewish believers in Jesus who find it almost impossible to refer to Jesus as "Christ" and to whom the words "cross" and "conversion" evoke thoughts of persecution and forced baptisms. Most missionaries to the Jewish people, therefore, prefer to use the terms "Messiah" instead of "Christ" and "Tree" instead of "Cross". The Jewish authorities regard this as deceitful, but the title "Messiah" is, in fact, more authentically Jewish than "Christ" and, according to the New Testament, Jesus was executed on "the Tree".

The numbers at the Osler Street meeting never reached a high level, but some good contacts were established through the outreach. The only gentile who Ernest welcomed to the meetings was Eddie Cairns, a professor of higher mathematics at the University of British Columbia. Ernest knew Eddie from Belfast and the Jewish people in the group liked him because of his academic brilliance and firm grasp of biblical Hebrew.

In addition to missionary work, Ernest represented the

International Jews Society at churches around Vancouver, and some of his meetings were advertised in the local newspapers. One Saturday evening, he received a telephone call from Peter Rothbart, a doctor at the Shaunessy Hospital in Vancouver. Dr Rothbart had seen an advertisement announcing that Ernest was to speak the next evening at New Westminster Presbyterian Church. Dr Rothbart was Jewish and wanted to know if Ernest would object to him attending the meeting. Ernest had no objection, but he warned the doctor that he would probably not like what he heard.

The Shaunessy Hospital was close to Osler Street and Dr Rothbart offered to take him to the New Westminster church. He picked up Ernest and Jessie and on the way to the church they spoke very little. Dr Rothbart sat with Jessie during the service and listened intently to Ernest's talk. After the service, he invited Ernest and Jessie to his apartment. He had many questions, particularly about what Ernest had said that evening. "I thought you were a Christian," he commented, "but you're very Jewish at heart. The rabbis tell us that Jews who become Christians become anti-Semitic."

At two thirty the next morning, he drove Ernest and Jessie back to the mission house and called later that day to ask if he could meet them again for a meal. When Dr Rothbart arrived, Ernest showed him into the lounge and excused himself to take a phone call. As he was speaking on the phone, Ernest heard an exclamation from the lounge. He returned to find the doctor with a copy of the IJS Herald. The reports of missionary work in the magazine were intended for supporters of the mission and not for Jewish people (even so, some misguided supporters still insisted on passing it to their Jewish friends), and Ernest feared Peter had been offended by something in the magazine. He apologised for leaving it where the doctor could pick it up.

It was not the written material that had surprised the young doctor but a picture of one of the BJS missionaries in South Africa, Dr Brian Pockroy. The two doctors had been boyhood friends and lived next door to each other in Northern Rhodesia, now Zambia. Brian Pockroy's father was a surgeon and Peter's father a general practitioner. They celebrated their Bar Mitzvahs on the same day, in the same synagogue, and grew up together.

"Have you heard anything about him lately?" Ernest asked.

"Oh yes." said Dr Rothbart. "He's got a bit odd."

"Like me?"

The young doctor blushed. Ernest asked if Brian had gone down in his estimation because he had become a believer in Jesus. Dr Rothbart was sorry that his childhood friend had forsaken the faith of his fathers, but he still held him in high esteem.

Almost twenty years later, Peter Rothbart is a medical consultant and remains a staunch friend of Ernest, writing to him at least twice a year. Ernest was invited to Peter's wedding and when he visits Vancouver he often stays with the Rothbart family. On one of Ernest's more recent visits, as the family were sitting at the meal table, Peter's teenage daughter asked why her father didn't believe the same as "Uncle Ernest". Her embarrassed father answered that it was an issue he and "Uncle Ernest" would have to talk about. In the privacy of his study he confided that he felt what Ernest said about Jesus was true, but if he became a Christian the shock would kill his parents.

*****

Throughout his missionary career, most of the Jewish objections to Jesus that Ernest encountered originated from

Jewish religious tradition. But this was now the Sixties, a decade of change when everything traditional was being questioned, and the Jewish community was not spared the intellectual challenges. A Christian lady in Vancouver introduced Ernest to a psychology student from a devout Jewish family, and the three had lunch together. The girl was highly intelligent and had been impressed by the book *We Have Reason to Believe*, written by the controversial Rabbi Louis Jacobs, the foremost British representative of the Masorti, or Conservative, wing of Judaism.

In its way, *We Have Reason to Believe* was to the Jewish community what J.A.T. Robinson's *Honest to God* was to the Christian world, and it may be helpful to outline the background to the book in order to understand the effect it had. In the first half of the twentieth century Anglo-Jewry was mainly Orthodox, though its ministers tended to be tolerant of other views. In the nineteen fifties, however, a cartel of rigidly Orthodox rabbis began to demand an "all or nothing" acceptance of Orthodox Jewish doctrine. Rabbi Jacobs was the foremost figure in the developing Conservative movement, and although he held the Bible in high regard, in *We Have Reason to Believe*, he vigorously contended that the entire Hebrew Bible, including the books of Moses, was susceptible to investigation with all the resources of modern knowledge. This flew in the face of the traditional Orthodox doctrine of *Torah haShamayim*, "the Torah from heaven", and a crisis occurred in 1962 when the Chief Rabbi and the London Beth Din – the rabbinic court – refused to sanction the appointment of Dr Jacobs as principal of Jews' College, on grounds of heresy. Two years later the Chief Rabbi, Israel Brodie, refused to allow Dr Jacobs to be reappointed as minister of his former congregation, the New West End Synagogue, because he denied the divine origin of the Torah.

An angry public row followed, after which most of the New West End Synagogue's members resigned and formed the New London Synagogue, with Louis Jacobs as its rabbi.

Rabbi Jacobs's book had impressed the young student. Jacobs was an urbane intellectual who refused to take Jewish dogma at face value. He wanted a Judaism that was founded on reason and took into account the discoveries of modern science. Ernest asked the student if now, having read *We Have Reason to Believe*, she was any further advanced in her knowledge of God and what he required of her.

She was bewildered. Though the orthodoxy of her parents did not satisfy her, she was afraid of drifting from Jewish observance and becoming assimilated into gentile society and culture. Her dilemma was identical to that of many Jewish young people. Tradition had ensured the survival of the dispersed Jewish people; it imbued them with a sense of identity and belonging in the face of persecution, deportation and the threat of extinction. However, to the modern Jewish mind, the tradition that had ensured the survival of the nation was wedded to folklore and pre-scientific concepts of the world. To reject the venerated traditions would seem to be a denial of the very thing that made her Jewish; to blindly accept the words of the Sages would be to commit intellectual suicide. The young academic was longing to know if there was a way that was right, a way that would satisfy her deepest needs and desires. Before Ernest could say anything, she looked at him: "I know what you are going to say – Jesus is the way. Jesus satisfies. But that doesn't work with me."

Ernest asked how she could know Jesus didn't "work" if she had never tried him. He asked if she had ever given Jesus any real consideration. As much as she had given Moses, Abraham or Ghandi, she said. Ernest could see that although he appeared to be making little headway with the girl, she was deeply troubled. What exactly was troubling her? Was it simply that times were changing and she was confused by the intellectual and religious climate? She replied that she had a deep dissatisfaction within her.

"That is the very need our Messiah, the Lord Jesus, can meet."

The look she gave him said she wanted to continue the conversation but another part of her knew she could not bring herself – despite the deep feeling of discontent – to abandon the traditional Jewish attitude to Jesus.

In addition to his work as an evangelist, Ernest preached extensively in Canada and the USA, travelling as far as Texas for meetings. In the churches of Victoria, the chief city on the deeply wooded Vancouver Island which lies opposite the city of Vancouver, Ernest found a great deal of encouragement. Many Christians rose to his challenge to reach out with the gospel to their Jewish friends and neighbours. In contrast to many other places where he had spoken, the churches of Victoria were concerned for the present spiritual welfare of Israel rather than the nation's future prospects. The people he met sought his advice about how they should approach their Jewish friends and colleagues with the Good News of Jesus the Messiah. What should they say? What should they not say?

Ernest's Canadian itinerary was extensive and the pace of life hectic. Towards the end of their time in Vancouver, in spite of the evident blessing of God on the visit, Jessie succumbed to the strain and had to be hospitalised.

*****

In 1969, Elie Nessim was appointed to the work in Vancouver. Elie had been born in Kobe, Japan, and raised in traditional

Judaism, being Bar Mitzvahed at the age of thirteen and attending synagogue each Sabbath and at the festivals. The family moved to the UK in the early fifties, and through the witness of a schoolfriend, Elie began to think about Jesus. It became clear to Elie that if Jesus was truly the Son of God and had risen from the dead, it must be a sin of enormous magnitude to reject him. The prophecy of the virgin birth in Isaiah 7:14 became pivotal in Elie's experience. He was convinced that the verse referred to the birth of Jesus and he committed himself in faith to the Immanuel who was born of the virgin.

Elie began work with the International Jews Society at the Gilead Medical Mission in Spitalfields, the very place where Ernest had begun his work thirty years previously. However, in the early 1960s the work in Spitalfields was in decline. The Jewish population of the East End had been rapidly decreasing since the end of the Second World War, and with the advent of the National Health Service there was little need for medical missions. In 1969 Elie, his wife Judith and their three children, Benjamin, Daniel and Rebecca, became the permanent residents of the mission house in Osler Street, Vancouver.

Ernest spoke at Elie's welcome meeting in Vancouver that year. He took as the basis of his address John 1:6 & 7: "There was a man sent from God…as a witness". He cautioned Elie and Judith not to expect quick results in Jewish mission but, instead, to do the work with God-given determination. "Elie, Judith and I," he told the congregation, "can speak from the inner circle; we have Jewish blood in our veins and we cannot, therefore, be accused of looking at things from the outside. There are times when our own people make cruel slurs against us, they accuse us of being in the work for money. They pour ridicule. This is the time when the love of Christ, shed abroad in our hearts, towers above everything else."

In build and personality, Elie and Ernest were opposites. Elie was small, slight and quietly spoken. Spiritually, they were both fearless in the cause of the Messiah, and the Jewish community was soon aware of Elie and the Bible Testimony Fellowship. His first approach to the work was to visit the Jewish leaders and synagogues. By 1974, the BTF was self-supporting, and in the eighties, through Elie's efforts, the Vancouver Messianic Fellowship was established. The VMF is a fine example of what a balanced messianic fellowship should be. It meets on the Sabbath but ninety per cent of the fellowship also attends a church on Sunday. In 1993, the Bible Testimony Fellowship became independent of CWI, but Elie has continued to maintain a bold evangelistic witness through the BTF and the Vancouver Messianic Fellowship.

14
Fisher of Men

Follow me, and I will make you
fishers of men. (Matthew 4:19)

In late 1965, Ernest delivered an address based on the words of Jesus: "I will make you fishers of men." He began with a quote from an anonymous source: "Jesus made saints and servants of fishermen who would otherwise have died in absolute obscurity in Capernaum without anyone except their neighbours being aware of them." The words might easily be applied to Ernest himself. The abandoned Jewish orphan who, under less favourable circumstances might have lived and died in obscurity among the millions who lived and worked in the British capital, had been called to be a saint and a servant of the Most High God, and was now a preacher of international repute.

He and Jessie had just returned to the UK after a gruelling world preaching tour that had taken them to Bermuda, Canada, New Zealand and Australia. The first stop in his itinerary had been the millionaire's paradise of Bermuda, to which he had been invited by a group of Christian businessmen. Far from the stopover affording a holiday, Ernest addressed 51 meetings in seventeen days, speaking some days as many as five times and starting as early as 6 o'clock in the morning. Eighty per cent of his meetings were with Brethren assemblies, but one of the most outstanding meetings was a Businessmen's Breakfast scheduled for 7.30 one Saturday morning. After breakfast, he spoke about the work of the BJS to an ethnically mixed group of Christian executives and their wives. They responded warmly to the news of the work and from that time on they supported the work both financially and in prayer. In 1998, Ernest said of that initial visit to Bermuda, "I had to work hard but in all the meetings I felt I was producing a prayerful interest in the Lord's work through the society, and only three weeks ago I had a letter from a Mr F. Barrett saying he'd never forgotten the visit, that never a day goes by when he doesn't pray for the mission and the missionaries".

While on the island Ernest was invited to appear on the popular Bermuda television programme, *Date Before Dinner.* He remembers being interviewed by "a very charming lady and a man but unfortunately neither of them seemed to know the Saviour and therefore they could not make head nor tail of what I was".

The host and hostess were used to talking to visiting politicians and businesspersons. This was the first time they had had a Hebrew Christian on the show, particularly one who, being so unfamiliar with television protocol, spoke plainly with no consideration for political correctness. The interview must have made interesting viewing as the bemused hostess admitted she had no idea there were such people as Jewish Christians. To her, one was either Jewish or Christian.

Ernest responded by asking if she knew what a Christian was. She thought people were born Christians. Ernest explained that he was Jewish by birth because his parents were Jewish. The lady and gentleman interviewing him were *Goyim* – gentiles – because their parents were gentiles. But no one is born a Christian. Not even going to church makes one a Christian. The bemused interviewers listened while their guest proceeded to spell out the biblical teaching about sin and grace, that race does not confer grace and that everyone – Jew or gentile – must trust in the death of the Messiah for salvation.

The interview was almost over when a piece of paper with a message was handed to Ernest requesting him to phone the American Naval Base and "ask for Jimmy". Jimmy was an officer in the United States Navy serving on an aircraft carrier. He was Jewish, and after watching *Date Before Dinner* Jimmy wanted to talk to Ernest. They met the following Saturday and Jimmy confided immediately that he was "in absolute confusion". Religiously, he and his spouse were like Jack Spratt and his wife. Jimmy's wife was a Roman Catholic, but they never talked about religion. He would not attend church with her and she would not go to synagogue with him. His confusion had been heightened by something that had happened to his father. Jimmy had been brought up in a religiously observant home in Houston, Texas. His father was so strict that he would not allow Jimmy and his sister to have Christian friends or even attend Scripture lessons at school. However, when Jimmy had last visited the family home his father was different. Within minutes of his arrival his father informed Jimmy that he had "met the Messiah". He had become a believer in Jesus and, as he put it to his son, he had "come as a lost sinner to a very wonderful Saviour".

"What am I going to do?" Jimmy asked. "My wife is a Roman Catholic, my father who brought us up to love Judaism and to be observant has turned Christian. And then, to make matters worse – or maybe better – I turned on the television and you appeared!" Before Ernest left the island he and Jimmy met several times and they remained in touch. After his father died, Jimmy wrote Ernest a very moving letter to say that he was reading the New Testament. Ernest's advice was to not talk to others about what he was reading but, instead, to read the New Testament for himself and, if he had any questions, to write to him.

On future visits to the island, Ernest would have further contact with Jewish officers of the US navy. On one occasion, as he got up to speak, he noticed a high ranking officer sitting at the back of the hall. It was evident that he was Jewish, because only a Jew would retain his hat during an act of worship. The officer had been passing the church and noticed a poster advertising *Mr. Ernest Lloyd – Hebrew Christian*. He was curious and so went in. He did not agree with much that Ernest said, but he wanted to attend some of his other meetings. Ernest thought it would be more helpful if the officer attended only the events at which he would be preaching and teaching, rather than when he would be reporting about the work of the BJS. Each time he and Ernest met they argued the case for Christianity, with little apparent progress. The day before Ernest left Bermuda the naval officer admitted that although Ernest's defence of the faith had not convinced him of the truth of the gospel, the love he received from Ernest's Christian friends had impressed him.

The importance of loving people was reinforced by the experience of another Jew from the US navy. Ernest saw a young Jewish man enthusiastically singing in the congregation. It was obvious that the young sailor was a believer and Ernest approached him after the meeting to ask how he found the Messiah. The young man was the only Jew aboard his ship, and the chaplain had sought him out to tell him of the great love he had for the Jewish people. He hoped the sailor would look upon him as a friend and as someone to whom he could go with his problems. The chaplain's evident love won his heart and he was drawn to the Messiah.

Bermuda, with its clear waters and 300 beautiful coral islands, is a popular tourist attraction for American Jews, but the resident Jewish community on the island is small. According to official Jewish figures, there are 125 Jewish residents of mixed nationality living on the main island. Most Bermudan Jews are secular and there is no synagogue or communal building. A lay leader conducts Sabbath worship and a visiting rabbi celebrates the High Holy Day services. As a result of the *Date before Dinner* broadcast, Ernest was invited to a home on the island where he was met not only by his Jewish hosts but also by a half dozen of their American friends. The welcome was by no means warm; despite the hot sunshine outside, the atmosphere in the palatial residence was icy. One or two of the guests were of the opinion that no "decent Jew" would ever adopt a new religion without some financial consideration, and asked how much he had been paid to "convert". At this point his host broke in and said it was unfair to condemn a man before giving him the opportunity to set forth his defence. Ernest could see that his "brethren according to the flesh" had not even the vaguest notion of what it meant to be a Christian. Instead of setting before them the evidences of Old Testament messianic prophecy or expounding a portion of the prophets, he explained that, before anything else, a Christian was someone who had had an experience of the living Saviour. Ernest was with the group for the entire morning, and by the time he left they wanted to know if he would be able to return to talk further before their vacation ended and they returned to New York.

When Ernest and Jessie boarded their plane in Bermuda, the temperature was 80°F in the shade. When they disembarked in Toronto, which was in the grip of a Canadian winter, the temperature was 20° below zero. It was his fifth visit to the country. He and Jessie spent a memorable first weekend at the missionary-minded Calvary Baptist Church in the town of Oshawa, some forty miles east of Toronto on the north shore of Lake Ontario. It was a successful start to the Canadian tour. After the Saturday evening meeting many of the members, particularly young people, indicated an interest in becoming prayer partners with the mission. On the Sunday he spoke at three services, including a live radio broadcast, and was deeply moved by the level of giving. For many years after, the church continued to generously support the BJS.

The members of Calvary Baptist had a great concern for the salvation of the Jews and a number invited their Jewish friends to attend the evening service. When Ernest rose to speak, it was to address a congregation which included more than twenty Jewish people. At the close of the service, a couple asked if they could talk to him. The three went into an adjacent room where the couple informed Ernest bluntly that they were vigorously opposed to "converting Jews to another faith" and did not believe a word he had said. They had, they said, "a *Yiddisher kop*" – a Jewish mind – and, to the thoughtful Jew, the Gospel account of the virgin birth was nonsensical. Ernest had spoken of Jesus as the greatest revelation of God but, as far as Judaism was concerned, Moses had given the Law and Israel did not need another lawgiver. They wanted to know what proof there was that Jesus was the Messiah. God had given them minds to think and they were firmly convinced that when the fanciful language was stripped away, the claims for the messiahship of Jesus had no foundation.

Ernest listened patiently. When they finished, he told them that in order to answer their objections he would have to refer to the Bible. They didn't want to hear from the New Testament. Ernest assured them that he would only refer to the Hebrew Scriptures and asked how many Jewish people they knew who ever opened the pages of the Bible. They responded by saying that the Bible was read every Sabbath in the synagogue. Ernest agreed that Moses and the Prophets were read in synagogue every Sabbath, but for most Jewish people that was the sum total of their exposure to the Word of God. He pointed out that Christians not only read the Bible on Sundays at church but also were urged to read the Bible privately and with their families every day. The couple eventually left without apparently conceding that Ernest was right on any point.

The incident highlights the spiritual plight of the Jewish people. It has become a standard Jewish objection that, "Jews don't believe in Jesus," and in 1986, a few years before his appointment as Chief Rabbi of the United Kingdom, Dr Jonathan Sacks lamented that, for most Jewish people, Jewishness was more important than God. "Jewishness" rather than Judaism had become the religion of most Jewish people. His observation is well justified and is nowhere more evident than when Jewish people are confronted with the evidence for Jesus. Jewishness, which the apostle Paul considered to be of great benefit in every way, has ironically become the greatest barrier to Jewish people coming to Jesus. It is one thing to lead Jewish people to Jesus in their own Scriptures. They can be shown, for example, that Psalm 22 and Isaiah 53 foretell the crucifixion of Jesus. It is an entirely different matter, however, to get Jewish people to trust in him.

After Toronto, Ernest and Jessie flew to Thunder Bay on Lake Superior, the largest of America's Great Lakes, and from there to Edmonton in Alberta, where the winter night-time temperature plummets to 50° below zero. On the flight to Edmonton, Ernest began to feel ill and had trouble breathing. Upon arrival in Edmonton, his hosts, Mr and Mrs Greenhalgh, consigned him to bed immediately and called the doctor, who, after a thorough examination, diagnosed severe bronchial pneumonia and high blood pressure. He spent ten days in hospital, much of that time in an oxygen tent, until his breathing became normal again.

After Ernest was discharged from the hospital, the doctor called to check on his recovery. Dr Rosen was a diminutive man, half the size of Ernest, extremely affable and evidently Jewish. After examining Ernest, he asked if he was Jewish. Ernest said he was. The doctor enquired further if he was *frum?*

Ernest replied that he was a Hebrew Christian missionary and was in Edmonton to speak on behalf of his mission. The doctor responded that he did not share Ernest's views, but said he would visit again. On his final call the two men spoke for a long time. The doctor was Jewish but not Orthodox. He did, however, observe the high holy days of Rosh Hashanah (New Year) and Yom Kippur (the Day of Atonement) because, as he put it, everyone makes mistakes and Yom Kippur was an opportunity to wipe the slate clean. The doctor's attitude toward sin was typical of many Jewish people, that sin is not as serious as it is said to be in the Hebrew Scriptures. According to the Talmud, in the tractate *Rosh Hashanah*, at the Jewish New Year, "Three books are opened [in heaven] … one for the thoroughly wicked, one for the thoroughly righteous, and one for the intermediate. The thoroughly righteous are forthwith inscribed definitively in the book of life; the thoroughly wicked are forthwith inscribed definitively in the book of death; the doom of the intermediate is suspended from New Year till the Day of Atonement; if they deserve well, they are inscribed in the book of life; if they do not deserve well, they are inscribed in the book of death."

During the ten days from New Year to the Day of Atonement, Jewish people attempt to top up their store of good deeds in order to swing the heavenly balances in their favour. "On this account," says *Hilcoth T'shuvah*, the rabbinic volume dealing with repentance, "all the house of Israel are accustomed to abound in almsgiving, and in good deeds, and to be diligent in the commandments in the interval between New Year's Day and the Day of Atonement more than in all the year besides."

Ernest asked courteously what the doctor thought King David meant when in Psalm 51 he described himself as "conceived in sin" and "shapen in iniquity". He made the point that this was not the terminology of "mistakes and peccadilloes". The doctor had no adequate answer but he retained a professional bedside manner and remained calm. Eventually, he excused himself and said he had to go. When Ernest told him he was fully insured and asked for the bill, the doctor refused to take even a cent for his services; he assured Ernest that it had been a pleasure to treat him, but cautioned him that he must learn to live life at a slower pace.

*****

Many of Ernest's introductions to Jewish families were initially through a wife or mother. It is frequently the case that the member of the family who is most religious is the matriarch. Although Liberal Judaism allows women to be rabbis, Orthodox women have no religious duties to perform other than to light the Shabbat candles. They cannot participate in the synagogue service. Instead, they observe the service in the gallery provided for that purpose and talk amongst themselves. Nevertheless, the woman of the house will usually make sure that the high days and holy days are celebrated, the kosher regulations are observed, the Sabbath meal is ready on time, the Sabbath candles are lit precisely eighteen minutes before sunset on Friday and the appropriate Sabbath prayers are recited.

After he had fully recovered from his bout of pneumonia, Ernest was taken to a Jewish home in Edmonton. The lady of the household looked at him and announced, "There's no need to introduce him; he's Yiddish. Now, what I want to know is, why do Jewish people change?"

Ernest said that before he answered the question he would like to know something about her and the family. "We go to *shul* – at least I do," she said. "My old man isn't quite as *frum* as me."

An opinion common among Orthodox Jews is that the only Jews who depart from the faith are those who have been raised in non-observant surroundings and have never been truly exposed to Judaism. If apostates could only experience life in a proper Jewish family or know the joy of one Sabbath, they would never stray. The woman was determined to convince Ernest that he had departed from the faith of his fathers. She wanted him to see what it was like to be "really Jewish", by which she meant she wanted him to see how carefully she kept the rabbinic kosher regulations.

She considered herself a better Jew than Ernest and in the conversation around the meal table she became increasingly belligerent, until her husband stepped in and told her to leave Ernest alone. As far as he was concerned, Ernest had every right to his opinion, but his wife felt Ernest should not have "changed".

Her attitude illustrates the great fear many Jewish people

have that if they believe in Jesus they will cease to be Jewish. A frequent objection to the gospel is, "I was born a Jew and I'll die a Jew," and the Canadian anti-missionary Rabbi Immanuel Jacob Schochet states that every Jew knows conversion to Christianity is an act of treachery and betrayal. The irony is that there is no consensus among Jews as to what constitutes "Jewishness", except that Jews don't believe in Jesus. Some say Jewishness is biological, though one may convert to Judaism and be regarded as a Jew; others that a Jew is defined by nationality, even though Jews live in almost every country in the world; the more orthodox seek a religious definition, even though there are Jewish Buddhists and spiritualists, as well as Jewish atheists and agnostics.

As he has done throughout his life, Ernest denied that he had "changed" in the sense that he was no longer Jewish. He has always maintained that being a believer in the Jewish Messiah authenticates his Jewishness; he is a complete Jew. This way of expressing the matter seemed to appeal to the lady, and during his time in Edmonton he visited the home on several occasions and each time received a warm welcome.

15
International Hebrew Christian

*Even so then at this present time also
there is a remnant according to the
election of grace.* (Romans 11:5)

In addition to his roles as a missionary and a representative
for Jewish mission, Ernest has been a major figure in the
world of Hebrew Christianity, or Messianic Judaism, as it has
come to be known. Before considering the part he has played
in this significant movement, it may be helpful to examine
the history of the phenomenon that is the Messianic Jewish
movement.

It has been estimated that there are now more Jews who
believe in Jesus than at any time since the first century. The
calculation has been made not only by the Christian and
Messianic communities but also by a number of Jewish
authorities. Rabbi Tovia Singer, the charismatic founder and
director of Outreach Judaism, which seeks to protect Jewish
people from Christian missionaries, advertises his series of
taped anti-missionary lectures with the question: "Why have
more Jews become Christians in the last 19 years than in the
last 1900 years?"

The beginning of the phenomenal growth in the number of Jews who believe in Jesus can be traced back to the mid-nineteenth century and the formation of missions to the Jewish people, which included the British Society for the Evangelisation of the Jewish People and the Barbican Mission to the Jews. In the decades following the launch of these societies, thousands of Jewish people became followers of Jesus, including such distinguished figures as Alfred Edersheim, the author of *The Life and Times of Jesus the Messiah*; David Baron, founder of the Messianic Testimony; Adolph Saphir, Anglican priest and author of several volumes, including a classic exposition of the Epistle to the Hebrews; Joseph Wolff, missionary to Moslems and Jews in the Middle East; Dr Leopold Cohn, founder of the American Board of Missions to the Jews; and Michael Solomon Alexander, the first Anglican Bishop of Jerusalem.

The first organisation to bring Jewish believers in England together was the *Benei Abraham* – "Sons of Abraham" – founded at Jews' Chapel in Palestine Place, London, on 9th September 1813. Faith in the Jewish Messiah, the Sons of Abraham claimed, made them "true Israelites".

However, the most significant moment in the history of the modern Hebrew Christian movement occurred a little more than fifty years later when, in 1866, Dr C. Schwartz, the Jewish minister of Trinity Chapel on the Edgware Road in London, called a number of fellow believers together to form the Hebrew Christian Alliance. By the turn of the century similar groups of Jewish believers had been established around the world and in 1925, the various national alliances came together to form the International Hebrew Christian Alliance and met at a conference in London.

So successful was the conference that Hugh Schonfield – once a professing Christian and missionary to his own people but later to become the notorious author of *The Passover Plot* – observed, "Since 1925, the history of Jewish Christianity becomes in effect the history of the IHCA." Such was the growth of the International Hebrew Christian Alliance that, prior to the outbreak of World War II, twenty national alliances were affiliated to the International Alliance.

Two years after the International Hebrew Christian Alliance conference, the President of the Alliance, Sir Leon Levison, wrote in the official organ of the IHCA, *The Hebrew Christian Quarterly*, that Jewish believers were distributed roughly as follows: 17,000 in Vienna; 35,000 in Poland; 60,000 in Russia; over 30,000 in the USA and Canada and 5,000 in the UK.

Ernest's introduction to the Hebrew Christian Alliance was through the Rev. Harcourt Samuel, who served the Alliance as its secretary for fifty years. They met in 1932 while Ernest was a student at All Nations College, and Samuel immediately took an interest in the young Jewish Christian and invited him to the family home in Buckinghamshire.

Ernest attended the 1934 International Hebrew Christian Alliance Conference at the Mildmay Centre in Stoke Newington. The conference was attended by some of the greatest names in the world of Hebrew Christianity, and the young man stood in awe of the gathered luminaries, which included Sir Leon Levison. Though dark and swarthy, with almost black eyes, Sir Leon was every inch a knight of the realm, resplendent in top hat and a swallowtail coat. Although English was his second language, he spoke it almost flawlessly, and was a first-rate orator.

Leon and his brother Nahum had grown up in the mountains of northern Galilee in the town of Safed, regarded by Orthodox Jews as one of Israel's four holy cities, along with Jerusalem, Hebron and Tiberias. Leon and Nahum's father was the rabbi of the oldest synagogue in Israel, and though devoutly Orthodox, he sent his sons to be educated in Edinburgh, where Leon came to faith in Jesus and soon after became a missionary to the Jewish people with the Church of Scotland. Nahum became a Church of Scotland minister in Leith.

Sir Leon was a visionary. In 1933 he purchased 2,000 dunams (200,000 square metres) of land near Gaza and told the 1934 conference about his dream of establishing a Hebrew Christian kibbutz in Palestine. He had shared his vision in a letter to the Hebrew Christian Alliance of America, dated 27th May 1933:

> I feel that in having Hebrew Christians to work upon the land in the very midst of the Jews who are returning to Palestine we shall have a constant living sermon that will be more effective than a million addresses delivered by word of mouth. It is only Hebrew Christians who love our people and the land, who will, therefore, be sent out.
>
> The future implications of the colony are full of immense possibilities and are pregnant with wonderful promises because settling 30 to 40 families on the land we shall be of necessity, required to build a house of worship and this will be the first Hebrew Christian Church in the Holy Land.

As self-sufficient workers on the land, the Jewish believers would not be perceived as "missionaries"; they would be part of the Zionist movement, working to build a homeland and safe haven for their increasingly oppressed fellow Jews in Europe. Ernest was gripped by Sir Leon's dream. For Ernest, the prospect of living in a Christian community in the land of his fathers became his dream also. But it was not to be. Fahmy Bey El Husseini, from whom Sir Leon purchased the land, refused to hand it over and kept the deposit. It was not until 1942 that the IHCA was able to recover the money, but by then Sir Leon was dead. The vision had foundered and Ernest found his calling in a life-long ministry to the Jewish people in the diaspora.

The man who had the most powerful impact on Ernest at the 1934 conference was Arnold Frank. When Ernest met him, Frank was in his mid-seventies and still an active missionary. His background was Jewish Orthodoxy, but in 1876, through the witness of a Christian friend, he became convinced that Jesus was the Jewish Messiah and was baptised. With the help of the Rev. J.D. Aston of the Irish Presbyterian Mission he trained in Belfast for the Christian ministry, and after his ordination in 1884 he returned to Hamburg to work under the auspices of the Jerusalem Church Mission.

Frank arrived in Hamburg at a time when thousands of Russian and Polish Jews were fleeing the harsh conditions and persecutions of Eastern Europe, seeking work or hoping to make their way to America. It was among these Jewish refugees from Russia and Poland that Frank did some of his greatest work. He provided food and accommodation for many of the indigent and penniless Eastern European Jews who daily arrived by ship and train. Leon Levison himself had been one of Arnold Frank's team in Hamburg, and it was for his work among the Russian refugees that King George V honoured Levison with a knighthood.

During his 54 years of service in Hamburg, Frank led hundreds of Jews to their Messiah, over fifty of whom became ministers or missionaries. In the first three decades of the twentieth century, when the British Jews Society needed suitable Jewish Christian missionaries for the UK, someone from the Jerusalem Mission invariably filled the post. A worker from the Jerusalem Church Mission came trained, seasoned and ready to begin work and, until the end of the thirties, almost half the missionaries in the British Jews Society originated from Hamburg.

*****

Ernest joined the Hebrew Christian Alliance in 1934, but it was more than twenty-five years before he held any official position within the movement. He was elected to the committee of the British Alliance in 1962 and became its president in 1977. The duration of each term of office was five years, and until Ernest's election no president had ever served more than one term. He was elected president on three consecutive occasions. He had earned a reputation for being a peacemaker and an encourager. In sessions of the council, when the discussion was becoming a little too heated, Ernest had a "soft word" that invariably calmed the situation.

Ernest was unexpectedly appointed President of the International Hebrew Christian Alliance at its conference in Canada in 1984. The presidents of the various alliances nominated the president of the Argentine alliance for the position but, in an unprecedented action, the delegates rejected the nomination. An improvised plan was put into effect and, to Ernest's dismay, the American president announced that the US delegation would like him to take on the presidency of the International Alliance. The motion was speedily seconded and he received the overwhelming support of the assembled delegates.

Just as Ernest's appointment to the presidency of the IHCA took place in an unprecedented manner, so his time in office would also be different. He served a total of ten years as the president of the IHCA – two consecutive terms – something also previously unknown. He served his two terms at a crucial time in the history of the IHCA because of the growing influence of Messianic Judaism within the Alliance. For most of the twentieth century, Jews who believed in Jesus had called themselves Hebrew Christians or Jewish Christians.

There had been previous attempts in the history of the Alliance to take the movement in the direction of Messianic Judaism, notably that of Mark John Levy at the Third National Conference of the Hebrew Christian Alliance of America, at Pittsburg, Pennsylvania in 1917. Levy proposed that the Alliance affirm a stronger loyalty to its Jewish past by adopting some of the customs of Judaism. In retrospect, his proposals appear moderate, but the other delegates questioned whether, as followers of the Messiah, they were under the law in any way. Levy's resolution was roundly defeated.

Though Mark John Levy's proposals were rejected by the American alliance, elsewhere there was sympathy for Messianic Judaism. The offence that the term "Christian" generated amongst fellows Jews led some Jewish followers of Jesus to refer to themselves as "completed Jews" and, under the influence of a new generation, the Hebrew Christian movement began to undergo a gradual metamorphosis. The Holocaust and the founding of the modern State of Israel enabled a new sense of Jewish identity to develop, and the Hebrew Christian movement was not exempt from the changes that were taking place in the Jewish world. The younger generation of Jewish followers of Jesus felt that "Hebrew Christian" no longer properly defined them and, therefore, a more adequate form of expressing their Jewish identity and beliefs was needed. The term "Messianic Jew" grew in popularity, so that in 1975 at its conference in Grantham, Pennsylvania, the Hebrew Christian Alliance of America changed its name to the Messianic Jewish Alliance of America.

The Messianic issue generated considerable heat, and some of the meetings in the eighties were stormy. The older believers felt no sense of shame about the terms "Jesus", "Christ", "Church" or "Cross" and were not embarrassed to call themselves Hebrew Christians. The new generation of Jewish believers wanted (with some justification) to jettison the Hellenised terminology and nomenclature of the New Testament and return to what they considered a more pure faith. Therefore they referred to their Saviour by his Hebrew title, *Yeshua haMashiach* – Jesus the Messiah – and called themselves Messianic Jews. In addition to restoring a purer and more authentically Jewish form of Christianity, the proponents of the Messianic movement believed the adoption – or reclamation – of such terminology would help break down a traditional obstacle to Jews believing in Jesus, i.e., that a Jew who believes in Jesus ceases to be a Jew.

More controversial was the proposal that Jewish believers should form Messianic assemblies or synagogues, the worship of which would be that of the traditional synagogue – including the wearing of the *tallit* (prayer shawl) and *kippah* (skullcap), and the inclusion of traditional Hebrew prayers, modified to reflect their faith in Yeshua.

To the older men, who had suffered rejection by family, friends, synagogue and the Jewish community, this smacked of compromise. The younger men behind the new proposals were, in the main, from secular Jewish backgrounds or from Reformed synagogues. Men like Victor Buksbazen, who were raised in Orthodoxy, had no wish to "return to the *shul*" and vigorously opposed the attempt to – as they saw it – Judaize the faith. Marvin Rosenthal was particularly scathing. In an article that appeared in the quarterly magazine *Israel My Glory*, he fumed:

About five years ago, a lie got started, its authors called it Messianic Judaism, or a movement within Judaism for the Messiah. From the rabbinical point of view the movement is not Jewish. Though neither "fish" nor "fowl," it has enamored and gathered to itself a growing company of followers. Its appeal lies in the fact that Jews are invited to remain Jews and simply accept the Messiah...They are encouraged to observe Jewish holidays and ritual – and in some instances, to attend the Jewish Synagogue as a form of worship. That the leaders of messianic Judaism love the Lord Jesus, no one denies – that most are zealous and sincere is not at issue – but that much of their theology and methodology distorts the meaning of the New Testament is patently clear.

Ernest had strong views on the issue and from time to time appointed a deputy to the chair so that he could express his opinion. He saw a danger in the strong emphasis the Messianics were placing on outward ceremony and tradition. He was free in Christ and did not want return to what Paul called the "beggarly elements" of rabbinic Judaism. While he sympathised with the concern of younger Jewish believers to return to their "Jewish roots", he reminded them that the Judaism to which they wanted to return was not the religion of Moses and the Prophets. Traditional Judaism had been adulterated by many extra-biblical elements and many of its doctrines were developed in opposition to those of the Church. In his book *The Christian Effect on Jewish Life*, Rabbi Michael Hilton agrees:

Judaism as we know it is the religion of the rabbis – men who lived in a world in which Christianity had already been born, a fast changing world with many religions and sects. Both Judaism and Christianity had to come to terms with the destruction of Jerusalem by the Romans, the loss of Jerusalem, of the temple, of the sacrificial system – the loss of a whole way of life. Christians and Jews developed different responses, theologies and practices in response to these events. A detailed examination shows that the rabbinic theologies and practices are not necessarily older than the Christian ones – on the contrary, Judaism often developed and changed in response to Christianity.

Ernest's opinions commanded respect, and though the American contingent in the International Hebrew Christian Alliance was strongly pro-Messianic, it was their influence that ensured his second term of office as President.

Ultimately, the influence of the new generation prevailed, and during Ernest's second term of office, the IHCA became the International Messianic Jewish Alliance. Although he was far from happy with the developments, Ernest could see positive elements in the Messianic movement. Apart from other considerations, he recognised the movement was unstoppable and held no grudges. He attended *Messiah 1988*, a full-blown Messianic event organised by the Messianic Jewish Alliance of America, which included what was termed "Davidic worship", or dance. He was at that time the President of the International Alliance and was invited by the conference to share his thoughts. His comments were in the main encouraging and positive but contained hints of a warning:

> I think that, quite candidly, you have every reason to be grateful to the God of our fathers for the wonderful movement that is taking place. If I can pinpoint something on the present position of the American Alliance, it is this: the real movement of the Spirit of God.

In my lifetime and that of my contemporaries in the British alliance, it was very rare that a family would come to a knowledge of Yeshua. Here in America, I consider it amazing to see whole families united in the faith. This particular conference is predominantly a young people's movement, something that we of the older generation have been praying for, for years and years.

In this conference you have impressed us with your attitude to those of the past generation. You haven't swept us out of the window. You feel that by God's grace we have made our own contribution. I believe that when you go into the annals of your own Alliance's history, you will feel that those people of the past did lay a very solid foundation and it was probably their prayers that have resulted in this tremendous movement of God that you have experienced in the last twelve to fifteen years.

For the future, I would say without hesitancy that you are only at the beginning of this movement... Remember that none of us can afford to stand still. This movement will march forward. I sincerely pray and trust that you will realise in the future your responsibility to the whole body of the International Alliance. Some of our alliances worldwide are small. They need your prayers, support and sympathy. God has visited you now and I believe he will visit you again in the future. We all pray that this great advancement here in America will affect the whole movement worldwide. It is a tragedy when we begin to be insular in our outlook. I believe that if your Alliance will feel part and parcel of the many alliances then tremendous blessings will come in the future.

At the age of ninety, Ernest is one of the last remaining members of a generation of Jewish believers that were known as "Hebrew Christians". Though the world of Hebrew Christianity has changed dramatically, he holds the position of Vice-President Emeritus of the British Messianic Jewish Alliance and remains a member of the finance committee and general purposes committee for the International Messianic Jewish Alliance. He recognises that the sphere of influence within the Messianic world has been steadily moving from England to the United States, and his message to the new generation that will have to carry the torch of Messianic faith into the future is simple: "Whatever you do, keep your eyes on the Messiah. It's the Messiah that matters, not ceremony". His strongest criticism, however, is levelled at the growing number of gentile Christians who attend Messianic congregations and wear tallit and kippah. His warning to them is plain and forthright: "Don't play at Judaism!"

Over the years, in his capacity as the President of the Hebrew Christian Alliance of Great Britain and the International Hebrew Christian Alliance, he has received criticism from gentile Christians — sometimes in offensive terms — accusing the Alliance of a narrow, nationalistic spirit. It has been a source of grief to him that Christians who find nothing nationalistic or narrow about the existence of, for example, Chinese churches or black churches in western societies, object strongly to Jewish Christian fellowships. It has never been the purpose of the Alliance to rebuild the middle wall of partition which, Paul says, has been abolished in Messiah.

The Alliance was censured also because, in spite of the fact that gentile Christian spouses of members are automatically eligible for membership, no gentile may hold office in the alliance. Ernest's answer to such criticism is that to allow gentile believers the same status would dilute the distinct Jewish nature of the IHCA and it would no longer be a *Jewish* alliance.

In spite of the suspicion the Messianic movement generates in the Jewish community, few can ignore it. One rabbinic spokesman has grudgingly conceded that the Jewish community has "little hope of stemming what is fast becoming a Hebrew Christian reality". Rabbi Dan Cohn-Sherbok's *Messianic Judaism*, published in 2000, was the first major mainstream Jewish attempt at an even-handed assessment of the movement. Rabbi Cohn-Sherbok even called for Messianic believers to be accepted by the Jewish world as genuine Jews.

Whatever the future holds for Jewish believers in Jesus, in each generation there will always be, according to Romans II, "a remnant according to the election of grace", until the time when the remnant of Israel will become the fulness of the Jews. That will be the time when, says Paul, "all Israel shall be saved". According to the apostle, that event will have repercussions for the entire world. It will be "life from the dead"!

16
The Importance of Being Ernest

He is a chosen vessel unto me. (Acts 9:15)

The years leading up to Ernest's retirement were as busy as ever. With the children grown up, Jessie was able to accompany Ernest on several of his overseas trips and was able to support him more directly. On 14th January 1967, they set off on a world tour that took them to Canada, Australia, New Zealand, Canada again, the United States and Bermuda. They returned to the UK on 20th January 1968.

Ernest's workload was heavy, and the society eventually saw that his burden needed to be lightened. Murdo MacLeod, who succeeded Will Newton as director, wrote in 1970, "The work of deputation has been carried on mainly by Mr. Lloyd, who bears the great burden of this particular work. Indeed, when he came to me with his programme of work for this year I practically threatened him with a big stick if he didn't let up a little bit!"

In order to ease the burden of paperwork, two years prior to Murdo MacLeod voicing his concern, Linda Miller had been taken on as Ernest's secretary at the IJS headquarters in

Eastbourne. She arrived in the office on 7th October 1968, but did not meet her new boss until ten days later after he returned from a tour of deputation. In her diary for that date she wrote: "Met my boss, Mr. Lloyd – very nice – gave me 31 pages of shorthand!" The following day she noted: "Another pile of shorthand – 25 pages!"

While he was away, Ernest would dictate letters onto cassette tapes and post them to Linda, but he never quite developed the habit of checking the batteries. He would simply speak into the machine until the tape stopped. Consequently, as the power in the batteries drained, the tapes slowed down so that when they were played back at normal speed they were indecipherable. Linda called them "Mickey Mouse" tapes because the voice was high and fast. Many times she and Kay Herring, another member of headquarters' staff, would be convulsed with laughter by the fast, high pitched, unintelligible sounds emanating from the dictaphone. Nevertheless, Linda remembers Ernest as a very kind and considerate boss.

The strain of constant travel, late nights and early mornings, lack of adequate rest and overwork began to tell, and during his last ten years with the mission Ernest succumbed to an increasing number of illnesses. Throughout his life, he had suffered from a catalogue of ailments, including bronchitis, bronchial pneumonia, high blood pressure, ulcers and spinal problems. Ernest could take heat, but cold was a problem. Some winters had seen him laid up for weeks with respiratory related illnesses such as pneumonia and pleurisy. But there were serious problems lurking below the surface. In March 1969, it was discovered that he had a duodenal ulcer and he had to undergo surgery, which put him out of action for a number of months. Five years later, in 1974, before he travelled to New Zealand, Ernest felt unwell and underwent what he considered to be a thorough medical examination. The doctor diagnosed a gall bladder infection, prescribed an appropriate course of treatment and issued a clean bill of health for Ernest to travel to New Zealand. In Invercargill, Ernest was rushed into hospital to undergo surgery for another duodenal ulcer. The consultant who performed the operation was appalled that the UK doctor had misread the symptoms and had allowed Ernest to travel. During the operation the doctor discovered a number of scars from other ulcers that had healed themselves, and he dubbed Ernest a "worry guts". Ernest's condition was serious and he was out of action for the best part of three months, having to spend a month in hospital and another six weeks recovering. His nervous disposition had affected him more than he knew. A lifetime of emotional stress had finally caught up with him and he had payed the price.

*****

Ernest officially retired in 1978, but not before he and Jessie had completed a five month tour of New Zealand, Australia, Tasmania and the USA. They wanted to retire within the London area, but property was expensive, and they found themselves in Carlisle. It was not their ideal choice, but at least Carlisle was near to their beloved Lake District.

Ernest and Jessie celebrated their Golden Wedding in 1987, and at a special gathering of friends and family, their son Peter expressed the deep regard he had for his mother. He had never married, but if ever he did marry, it would have to be to someone like his mother. He, his brother Martin and their adopted sister Jennifer owed everything to her. Dad was away more than he was at home, Peter told the gathering, but although mother missed him, she never grumbled or complained. When the children sought her advice on a course of action, she would counsel them to ask themselves if it was worth doing. The same caution was given to others.

However, a shadow hung over the celebration. For some time, the once energetic and indefatigable Jessie had begun to tire quickly and the alert mind was evidently slowing down. The first alarming indication of how bad things were came while Ernest and Jessie were on holiday in the highlands of Scotland. They were staying at Clifton House in Kingussie, a place familiar to them both, but Jessie appeared not to know where they were. Worse still, after Ernest returned from a day of hiking in the hills, Jessie asked repeatedly why the hands on the clock were turning so quickly.

Their sons, Peter and Martin, had both lived in Northern Ireland for several years, and suggested that their parents move to be nearer them. The mission agreed to purchase a small bungalow at Portrush on the rugged North Antrim coast, not far from the Giant's Causeway. Jessie's condition continued to deteriorate, and for three years there was scarcely a night in which Ernest did not have to get out of bed three or four times to tend to her needs. The strain was no burden to him. She wasn't heavy; she was Jessie. Throughout the long years of their marriage Jessie had carried the responsibilities of bringing up a family and caring for an extended household, and Ernest felt it was a privilege to look after his now frail, elderly and disoriented wife. It was a small way in which he felt he could repay the debt he owed her.

When it became apparent that Jessie was in need of round-the-clock professional care and attention, she entered a nearby Presbyterian nursing home. The nurses were gentle and caring and looked after Jessie with tenderness, but the only person she allowed to take her out in her wheelchair was Ernest. The bond forged between them over 55 years became stronger in her final days. It was distressing for Ernest to see his once strong and capable wife utterly dependent on him. The last time Ernest saw Jessie, she asked him repeatedly to hold her hand. It was evident that she was close to death, but only Jessie herself knew how close. She had sensed for some days that the end was near and when her nurse said goodbye to her before going on holiday, Jessie replied, "You won't see me when you come back. Jesus is going to come for me this week and I'm going to be free. I'm just going to miss Ernest..." A few days later, on Sunday 10th May 1992, Jesus came for her and she was free.

The funeral service was attended by a large number of family and friends, Jewish and gentile. Hebrew Christian and CWI colleague Alan Sax paid tribute to Jessie's qualities, her love of reading and walking and her photographic memory, her generous and forgiving spirit, her ability to provoke thought and stimulate reflection, and her bluntness: "She said what she meant and she meant what she said."

*****

By any standard, the life of Ernest Lloyd has been remarkable, spanning, as it does, almost the whole twentieth century. He has lived through the reigns of five monarchs and under the leadership of twenty different Prime Ministers; he has experienced the trauma of two World Wars and has seen the gradual decline of the British Empire as well as the establishment and survival of the state of Israel.

Ernest has never owned his own home, never learned to drive, never learned another language and never sent an email. At the age of ninety, he has a better memory than some men half his age. He is an avid reader, a lover of music and an indefatigable writer of letters, all of them bashed out with remarkable inaccuracy on a series of manual typewriters, each of which he has worn out.

The mission Ernest has actively served for seventy years has changed its name twice – in 1965 the BJS became the International Society for the Evangelization of the Jews and, with the Barbican Mission to the Jews, in 1976 it became Christian Witness to Israel – and he has outlived five of its directors. In his three score years and ten of missionary service, Ernest has travelled more than a million miles by land, sea and air and preached more than 200,000 times in some twenty countries to countless multitudes. Although his pace of life is nowhere near as hectic as it was as a missionary, most years Ernest is away for three months on a preaching tour that takes him to Australia, New Zealand and Canada. He also serves on the councils of Christian Witness to Israel (in an honorary capacity), the International Messianic Jewish Alliance, the British Messianic Jewish Alliance and the Spanish Gospel Mission.

He is an evangelist, a teacher, a preacher, an advocate of mission to the Jewish people and a spokesman for the international Messianic movement. In spite of frequent bouts of ill health, he single handedly laid the foundations for the work of missions to the Jewish people in South Africa, India, Australia, New Zealand and Canada. Though not all remained affiliated to Christian Witness to Israel, almost all those branches continue to present a vibrant witness to the Jewish communities in their countries.

The number of Jews and gentiles who have been saved through his ministry, either directly or indirectly, is incalculable. In many cases he led them to Christ himself, but at other times his role was to break down prejudices and lay a foundation on which others could build or, to change the biblical metaphor, he broke up the fallow ground allowing others to sow and reap. The number of lives he touched for good by preaching, teaching, encouragement, advice, kind words and actions, example and precept cannot be counted.

It is in his role as an evangelist that one of Ernest's outstanding qualities is seen most clearly. An almost infinite patience has enabled him to suffer being rebuffed time after time in his efforts to lead his "kinsmen according to the flesh" to the Messiah. A notable example of his capacity to endure rejection in the cause of the gospel was when he called at the office of a Jewish company and asked to see the director. The moment Ernest introduced himself he was angrily ordered out of the building. After a cooling-off period of three weeks, Ernest returned. This time the director was livid with rage: "Don't you understand English? When I told you to get out, I meant it!"

Ernest quietly pointed out that Jewish people complain about the intolerance of the goyim, but this man was the most intolerant person he had ever met. He knew nothing about Ernest but he was not prepared to give him a fair hearing.

"I know what you're here for. You're out to destroy my religion!"

Ernest replied that that was not his intention.

"Come back at mid-day and we'll go out."

Ernest returned, and the two men went to a nearby restaurant for a lunch hour that lasted three and a half hours, during which the businessman did most of the talking while Ernest listened. As they parted, Ernest asked if they could meet again. He agreed, and when they next met he invited Ernest and Jessie to his home for a meal. It was a rough ride. The family was Orthodox and the food strictly kosher. The father was an officer in the synagogue and throughout the evening his four feisty daughters attacked Ernest mercilessly, berating him for forsaking the Jewish religion and thereby betraying his own people. He took their verbal blows on the chin and left the home emotionally bruised. But the friendship between the two men deepened, so that Ernest was allowed to visit the office any time he was in town. On one of his later visits, Ernest noticed the first volume of Dr Martin Lloyd-Jones' series of expositions of the Epistle to the Romans, *Atonement and Justification*, on his friend's desk. "I picked this up at a second-hand bookshop." he said. "I always thought the New Testament was a Christian book, but it's a Yiddisher book!"

Twelve years after their initial meeting, Ernest stepped onto a platform to preach and was amazed to see in the front row his old friend with his wife, their four daughters and their husbands. All of them were now believers in Israel's Messiah.

In his preaching and teaching, Ernest still exudes an authority and power that is gripping. When I was interviewing him for the purpose of writing this book, he accompanied me to a home group at which I was speaking. He sat at one end of the long, narrow living room and I at the other. Towards the end of my talk to the church group, I asked if he would like to add anything. Ernest is a big man, but as he began to speak it was as though he began to grow and fill the room. The eyes of everyone were fixed on him and I was entirely forgotten.

During the time this book was being written, Ernest preached at the church I attend. I thought he looked frail as he slowly made his way up the steps onto the platform. However, the appearance of frailty quickly disappeared as he began to speak; the stentorian tone of his voice carried an authority that soon had the congregation under his spell.

*****

Ernest is the last of a generation of Hebrew Christians that included men of the calibre of Mark Kagan, Victor Buksbazen, Herman Newmark and the Bendor-Samuels. Another generation of Jewish believers has arisen, many of them learned in rabbinic literature and zealous for the cause of Messianic Judaism. It should be our prayer that the new generation will feel the same deep love for their people and be willing to sacrifice as much for their salvation as Ernest has done. Nevertheless, it may be that other generations of Jewish believers will come and go before another appears who will play a role in the purposes of God as significant and important as that played by Ernest Lloyd.

Glossary

Aliyah. Hebrew: "Going up." Emigration to Israel.

Anti-semitism. The hatred of Jews for no reason other than that they are Jews.

Ashkenazi. A Northern or Eastern European Jew.

Bar Mitzvah. Hebrew: "Son of the Commandment." At the age of thirteen a Jewish boy reaches maturity and is called on to read the Torah portion at the morning service in the synagogue.

Benei Israelis. Hebrew: "Sons of Israel."

Beth Din. Hebrew: "House of Judgement." A Jewish court of law which officiates over religious matters such as *kashrut* and the granting of divorces.

B'rit HaDashah. Hebrew: "New Testament."

Chaim HaDashim. Hebrew: "New Life."

Eretz Yisrael. Hebrew: "The Land of Israel."

Erev Shabbat. Hebrew: "Sabbath Eve." Friday night when the traditional Sabbath meal is eaten.

Frum. A Yiddish word describing someone who is strict in religious observance.

Goy/Goyim. Hebrew: "Gentile"/"Gentiles."

Hadderech/HaDerekh. Hebrew: "The Way."

Hanukkah. Hebrew: "Dedication." The winter festival that

219

commemorates the victory of Judah Maccabee over the Syrians, and the dedication of the temple in Jerusalem.

Hasidim. Hebrew: "The Pious." The Hasidic movement began in Eastern Europe, with an emphasis on ritual purity, good deeds and joy.

HaTikvah. Hebrew: "The Hope." The national anthem of Israel.

Heder. Hebrew: "Room." An elementary school.

Kabbalah. Hebrew: "Received." A system of mystical teachings and practices which seeks to uncover the mysteries of God and his relationship to his creation.

Kibbutz. An Israeli agricultural collective.

Kibbutznik. A member of a kibbutz.

Kippah. A round skull cap worn by Orthodox men, also known as a *yarmulke.*

Kashrut. Hebrew: "Fitness." The laws governing whether food is *kosher* (fit) or *trayf* (unfit).

Mashiach. Hebrew: "Messiah."

Meshuganeh. Yiddish: "Mad."

Meshummad. Yiddish: "Apostate."

Mitzvah. A commandment, duty or good deed.

Pesach. Passover.

Philo-semitism. Love of the Jewish people; the opposite of anti-Semitism.

Rosh Hashanah. Hebrew: "New Year."

Sabra. A native Israeli. Like the cactus after which they are called, Israelis are hard and prickly on the outside but sweet and soft inside.

Shochet. Hebrew: "Butcher."

Schnorrer. Yiddish: a good-for-nothing, a scrounger or beggar.

Sephardi. A Jew of Spanish origin.

Shabbat. Hebrew: "Sabbath."

Sheeny. Slang. A contemptuous and insulting term for a Jew.

Shema. Hebrew: "Hear." The first word of the great confession of faith found in Deuteronomy 6:4: *Shema Yisroel, Adonai Eloheinu Adonai echad*: "Hear, O Israel, the Lord our God, the Lord is one."

Shul. Yiddish: "Synagogue."

Siddur. The Daily Prayer Book.

Sukkot. Feast of Tabernacles.

Tallit. Prayer Shawl.

Talmud. The written Oral Law; a monumental record of the discussions of the Jewish sages. It consists of wide-ranging discussions, folk-tales, prayers, proverbs and legal rulings. The entire Aramaic text runs to approximately two and a half million words.

Tanakh. The Hebrew Bible. Tanakh is an acronym for the three divisions of the Old Testament: *Torah* (Law), *Nevi'im* (Prophets) and *Ketuvim* (Writings).

Tefillin. Hebrew: "Phylacteries." Leather boxes containing portions of the law, based on Exodus 6:8, worn by Jewish men on the forehead and left arm at morning prayers.

Torah. Hebrew: "Teaching." The term is used in several ways by Jewish people. It can mean the five books of Moses, all the laws on a given subject, the entire law of God (consisting of 613 commandments), the Bible or the Oral Law.

Torah HaShamayim. Hebrew: "Torah from heaven." A term relating to the divine origin of the Law.

Yeshua haMashiach. Hebrew: "Jesus the Messiah."

Yiddish. The language of Ashkenazi Jews, it is written in Hebrew letters.

Yiddishkeit. Jewish culture.

Yom Kippur. Day of Atonement.

Zaddik. Hebrew: "Righteous man." A title given to Hasidic leaders.

Christian Witness to Israel

Christian Witness to Israel was formed in 1976 by the coming together of two missions—the Barbican Mission to the Jews and the International Society for the Propagation of the Gospel among the Jews—both of which had a history dating back to the mid nineteenth century. For all if its 160 year history, the society has been committed to telling Jewish people about Jesus.

Today, CWI has missionaries in the UK, Israel, Australia, Bulgaria, France, Hungary, and New Zealand.

Our main ministry in Israel is HaGefen Publishing, which produces high-quality evangelistic literature and books to help God's people grow in grace and in the knowledge of the Messiah. HaGefen is currently producing a beautifully illustrated edition of the Bible in modern Hebrew.

In the UK we have missionaries in Bournemouth, London, Leeds and Glasgow. Their methods of making contact with Jewish people vary. Home visits, door-to-door visiting, street evangelism and open-air preaching are just some of the ways used by CWI missionaries to tell Jews about Jesus. In Leeds, the Leeds Messianic Fellowship offers a culturally friendly setting where Jewish people can hear the Good News.

In Sydney, Australia there is a large Jewish community in Bondi, but in New Zealand the Jewish population is more thinly spread. Through the ministry of CWI workers in both countries Jewish people have found Jesus as their Messiah and Saviour.

There are still large Jewish communities in Eastern Europe and we have recently commenced a work in Budapest, the city where the BMJ began its ministry through the efforts of Dr John "Rabbi" Duncan.

The quarterly CWI *Herald* features reports by missionaries, and thought-provoking articles relating to Jewish mission and biblical understanding. It is sent free of charge to all who request it. There are two web sites, one providing information about the work of CWI (www.cwi.org.uk) and the other evangelistic (www.shalom.org.uk).

Christian Witness to Israel, 166 Main Road,
Sundridge, Sevenoaks, Kent, TN14 6EL.

Phone: 01959 565955. Fax: 01959 565966.
E-mail: hq@cwi.org.uk